It's All Perfect
What If Nothing in Your Life Was a Mistake?

Mardoche Sidor, MD
Karen Dubin, Ph.D., LCSW
SWEET Institute

SWEET Institute Publishing
Transformational Books for a Transformational World

Copyright © 2025 by SWEET Institute

All rights reserved. No part of this book may be reproduced, stored in a retrieval system, or transmitted in any form or by any means—electronic, mechanical, photocopying, recording, or otherwise—without the prior written permission of the publisher, except in the case of brief quotations embodied in critical articles or reviews.

Published by SWEET Institute Publishing
New York, NY

WWW.SWEETInstitutePublishing.com

First Edition
Printed in the United States of America

ISBN (Paperback): 978-1-968105-07-5

Library of Congress Control Number: 2025942589

Cover Design by SWEET Institute Publishing

Interior Design and Layout by SWEET Institute Publishing

For bulk orders, permissions, or media inquiries, please contact: contact@sweetinstitute.com

Unless otherwise noted, all stories and case examples in this book are either fictionalized or used with permission, and identifying details have been changed to protect the privacy of individuals.

SWEET Institute Publishing
Transformational Books for a Transformational World

Dedication

To everything that went wrong.
To every door that closed,
every heart that broke,
every moment that didn't go as planned.

To the confusion, the detours, the delays.
To the grief you didn't see coming.
To the silence that felt like abandonment.
To the versions of you that you outgrew.
To the chapters that didn't make sense—until now.

To the pain that cracked you open.
To the stillness that called you back.
To the knowing that kept whispering:
"This, too, belongs."

This book is dedicated to the whole of your life—
not just the healed parts,
not just the parts that made sense,
but all of it.

Because it was all perfect.
Because it still is.
Because you are.

Other Books by Mardoche Sidor, M.D; Karen Dubin, PhD, LCSW; with the SWEET Institute

- Journey to Empowerment
- Discovering Your Worth: Everything You Need to Feel Fulfilled
- The Power of Faith: A Harvard-Trained Psychiatrist Speaking on Faith
- The Psychotherapy Certificate Course: The Clinician and Coach Manual (Books 1–3)
- The Anxiety Course: The Workbook
- What's Missing
- NLP for Clinicians
- 50 SWEET Poems: Reflections on life, love and self
- The Power of Belief: How Ideas Shape Leaders, Nations and the Future
- The Courage to Care: Stories of Healing, Hope, and the Power of Social Work: Told by Over 50 SWEET Institute Social Workers
- Transforming Team Relationships from the Inside Out: The SWEET Healing Circle for Agencies: Redefining Accountability, Collaboration, and Culture
- Remembering: The Journey Back to the Pre-Conditioned Self
- The Clinician's Mirror: A Story of Projection, Self-Awareness, and Transformation for Clinicians
- The Secret Is in Remembering: Why We Suffer, Why We Forget, and How to Return to Who We Are

Table of Contents

Preface	7
Introduction	9
Why This Book	11
What This Book Is About	13
How to Use This Book	14
How This Book Works	16
Acknowledgments	18

PART I: THE FORGETTING — 19

- Chapter 1: It's All Perfect — 20
- Chapter 2: The Conditioned Self — 25
- Chapter 3: Why We Suffer — 30
- Chapter 4: The Myth of Control and the Fear of Uncertainty — 36
- Chapter 5: The Architecture of the Mind — 41

PART II: THE REMEMBERING — 47

- Chapter 6: The Preconditioned Self — 48
- Chapter 7: Meaning, Memory, and the Inner Map — 53
- Chapter 8: The Four Layers of Transformation — 58
- Chapter 9: Thought Is Not Reality — 64
- Chapter 10: Living from the Inside-Out — 70

PART III: THE RETURN   **76**

Chapter 11: Radical Acceptance and the Gift of Suffering   77
Chapter 12: From Behavior to Belief   83
Chapter 13: Free Association and the Wisdom of the Unconscious   89
Chapter 14: The Existential Compass   94
Chapter 15: Integration – A Life Remembered   100

Closing Poem   **105**

Epilogue: The Still Point   **106**

Conclusion: There Was Never Anything Wrong With You   **108**

Invitation to the Reader   **110**

Final Acknowledgments   **113**

Reader Integration Toolkit   **114**

Appendices   **117**

About the Authors   **134**

Preface

By Mardoche Sidor, MD

I was taught to work hard, to fix what's broken, and to keep moving forward. Like so many of us, I believed progress was linear, healing was a destination, and anything that didn't go according to plan was a problem to be solved.

But over time—through psychiatry, psychoanalysis, conscious inquiry, and my own deep undoing—I began to see something else.

I began to see that what we call "problems" are often portals. I began to see that the things we think we need to change are often the very things trying to change us. I began to see that the pain we spend our lives avoiding is not the enemy—it's the invitation.

I began to realize that nothing had gone wrong.

And so this book was born from a deeper remembering—one that emerged slowly, and then all at once:

It's all perfect.

Not because life is easy.
Not because trauma is justified.
Not because suffering should be idealized or minimized.
But because every single moment—when seen through the eyes of wholeness—is part of the unfolding.

In this book, we explore that unfolding together; and not through ideas alone, but through practice, reflection, and the application of a model that I've spent my whole life refining: The 4 Layers of Transformation.

We begin with the conscious—the layer of habits, behaviors, and routines.

We descend into the preconscious—the realm of beliefs, schemas, and emotional patterns.

We courageously enter the unconscious—the layer of repressed memories, buried wounds, and unspoken truths.

And we arrive, finally, at the existential layer—where we remember that we are free, we are choosing, and we are already whole.

Each of these layers is essential. Each must be visited, felt, worked through, and integrated. And when they are, healing is no longer a goal. It becomes a state of being—a way of remembering.

It's All Perfect is not a book of advice.
It is not a book of answers.
It is a mirror, a map, and an invitation.

Whether you are a clinician, an inquirer, a leader, or someone simply trying to make sense of life—this book is for you.

Because eventually, if you stay present long enough,
if you slow down enough,
if you remember who you were before the world told you otherwise—
you, too, will see:

It was all perfect.
Even this.

—Mardoche Sidor, MD
Founder, SWEET Institute
Medical Director, Urban Pathways
Columbia University Center for Psychoanalytic Study and Research
Clinician, Teacher, Student

Introduction

By Karen Dubin, PhD, LCSW

For years, I searched for the most effective treatment approaches for my clients—constantly learning, testing, and adjusting to see what might help them feel better, function more effectively, and experience greater satisfaction in life. I believed that healing meant identifying the right method and applying it perfectly in order to fix what was wrong.

But over time, I began to see something different. Despite all the techniques I used, the most meaningful change seemed to come not from the intervention itself, but from the presence. The relationship. The remembering.

This book was born from that remembering.

What if nothing had gone wrong?

What if every moment was exactly as it needed to be—even the ones we would never wish on anyone?

What if the broken places weren't barriers, but beginnings?

It's All Perfect is not a naïve declaration. It's a radical reframe. A call to stop fighting the story and start listening to it. A call to stop trying to control life—and start partnering with it.

This book introduces a layered model of transformation that goes far beyond surface change. It invites you to engage your life across the conscious, preconscious, unconscious, and existential levels—so that healing isn't something you chase, but something you uncover.

This is a book about perception and peace, about truth and trust. It's a book about reconnecting with who you are.

It's for the clinician who wants to go deeper, the leader who wants to live more authentically, the individual who is ready to turn pain into purpose.

Above all, this book is a reminder:
That you are not broken.
That nothing was wasted.
That everything belongs.
And that the life you're living—even now—is part of a perfection greater than you can see.

Welcome to the remembering.
Welcome to the work.
Welcome to the wonder.

It is all perfect.
Even this.

—Karen Dubin, PhD, LCSW
Co-Founder, SWEET Institute
Co-Author, SWEET Institute Publishing
Clinician. Educator. Explorer of Meaning

Why This Book

Because we forget.

We forget that healing is possible.
We forget that clarity is natural.
We forget that what happened to us isn't the end of the story—it's part of becoming aware.
We forget that even the most painful moments have the power to bring us closer to who we really are.

This book is here to help you remember.

It's here for the part of you that has always known—quietly, patiently—that there is a deeper order at work. That beneath the chaos, beyond the confusion, everything is unfolding with intelligence, intention, and meaning.

It's here because our world is loud with urgency, full of fear, and addicted to fixing what was never broken in the first place. And it's time we said something different.

It's All Perfect doesn't mean we don't take action.
It doesn't mean we minimize trauma or bypass suffering.
It means we begin with the radical recognition that nothing is wasted.
That every moment is precious.
That even pain can be a portal.

This book exists to bridge the gap between intellectual insight and embodied change.
It brings together science and soul, psychoanalysis and presence, practical tools and poetic truths.

It invites you to walk the 4 Layers of Transformation:

- Conscious change—habits, routines, behaviors.
- Preconscious insight—schemas, beliefs, patterns.
- Unconscious healing—repression, trauma, memory.
- Existential integration—freedom, purpose, meaning.

Because true healing isn't linear. It's layered.

You are not just here to survive. You are here to remember.
To reclaim.
To live fully.

That's why this book exists.

Because it's time.
Because you're ready.
Because it's all perfect—even this.

What This Book Is About

This book is about transformation—not just the kind you talk about, but the kind you live. The kind that doesn't just change your mind, but your whole experience of reality.

It's about seeing what's been there all along. The pattern beneath the pain. The meaning beneath the mess. The wisdom within the wound.

It's about remembering what you forgot—not because you weren't paying attention, but because the world taught you to forget.

It's about the four layers of transformation:
- The Conscious Layer, where habits, behaviors, and structure help you regain your footing.
- The Preconscious Layer, where beliefs, schemas, and inner narratives begin to surface.
- The Unconscious Layer, where repressed experiences and hidden truths find the light.
- The Existential Layer, where freedom, meaning, and personal responsibility come alive.

This book is about learning to see every moment—even the painful ones—as part of the perfect unfolding of your life.

It's about perception and presence.
Integration and insight.
Awareness and action.

It's a guide, a practice, a framework, and a mirror.

And more than anything, it's an invitation:
To stop trying to fix what isn't broken.
To stop resisting what's already working.
To start remembering what you already know.

It's all perfect.

Even this.

How to Use This Book

This book is not meant to be read once and put away. It's meant to be lived, revisited, and practiced.

Each chapter invites you into a journey—through insight, reflection, and implementation. You will move through the 4 Layers of Transformation: Conscious, Preconscious, Unconscious, and Existential. Each layer is essential. Each one builds on the next.

Here's how to use this book:

1. Read Slowly.
Let the words land. This book is written in a dialogue-based, conversational style. Pause when something moves you. Sit with what stirs discomfort. Let the process be nonlinear.

2. Engage the Tools.
Every chapter includes visuals, infographics, exercises, and tools—designed to move you from understanding to integration. Use them. Reflect on them. Return to them.

3. Practice the Prompts.
You'll find questions, commitments, and invitations for each chapter. They're not optional. They're the doorway to change.

4. Notice Your Resistance.
If something feels hard, it's likely important. Don't skip the sections that challenge your current beliefs. That's where the real shift begins.

5. Use the SWEET Topographical Model.
This book is grounded in the SWEET Institute's 4-layer model of change. Refer to the visual guides often. Apply the model to your own patterns. Share it with others.

6. Come Back Again.
Healing is layered. Integration takes time. You may find that a chapter means something entirely new months from now. That's not regression. That's growth.

This is more than a book—it's a companion on your journey home to yourself.

You don't need to be perfect.
You only need to remember:
It already is.

Even this.

How This Book Works

This book works by engaging all parts of you—your mind, your emotions, your body, and your deeper knowing.

It's structured around the SWEET Institute's 4 Layers of Transformation:

1. **Conscious Layer** – The surface layer: habits, routines, behaviors, structure, discipline. This is where behavior change begins.

2. **Preconscious Layer** – The hidden patterns: schemas, beliefs, core narratives, attachment, and emotion regulation. This is where you start to see what's been shaping your reactions.

3. **Unconscious Layer** – The repressed: memories, trauma, defense mechanisms, and symbolic material like dreams and slips. This is where deep healing occurs.

4. **Existential Layer** – The truth of who you are: freedom, choice, responsibility, meaning, and connection to a greater whole. This is where everything integrates and becomes real.

Each chapter is crafted to guide you through these layers, using a consistent structure:

- **Dialogue-Based Narrative**: We speak directly to you. You're not just reading—you're in conversation.

- **Scientific Insights**: Grounded in evidence-based therapies and neuroscience, with full citations and references.

- **Visual Tools**: Diagrams, infographics, and models to help you see what words alone can't explain.

- **Prompts & Reflections**: To move you from thought to insight to transformation.

- **Commitments & Practices**: Small, daily steps to support sustainable change.

- **Integration Checkpoints**: Opportunities to pause, review, and connect the dots across the layers.

The more actively you engage, the more powerful your results. This isn't about reading and knowing. This is about remembering and becoming.

The more you bring your life into these pages, the more these pages will bring life into you.

This book works because you work—with intention, with honesty, with courage, and with the deep inner knowing that it's all unfolding just as it should.

It's all perfect.
Even this.

Acknowledgments

"We thought it had to go differently. But it went exactly as it needed to."

This book was shaped by what didn't work out, by the plans that fell apart, the starts and stops, the questions that had no answers, the people who came, left, or changed, the chapters we resisted—until we saw they were the ones that transformed us. It is because of all of that—not in spite of it—that this book came to be.

To every delay, detour, disappointment, and disruption: Thank you. You were not obstacles. You were architects.

To the SWEET Institute family—your commitment to healing through presence, depth, and practice made these pages possible. You remind us that transformation doesn't happen when everything is easy. It happens when we remember who we are, especially when it's not easy.

To our patients, clients, students, and community—you are the proof that this work matters. You've taught us that remembering is possible—even in the midst of chaos.

To those who supported us, stood by us, or challenged us—you were all part of the perfection. We needed you, even when we didn't know it yet.

And to you, dear reader: You found this book at the right time. You are in the right place. You are not behind. Nothing went wrong. It's all perfect. Even this.

PART I: THE FORGETTING

Chapter 1: It's All Perfect

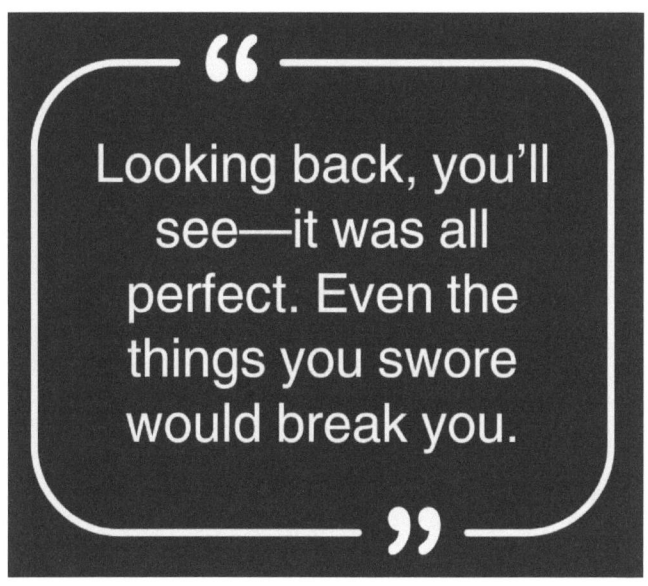

Maya: I don't understand. How can you say it's all perfect? My life is chaos. Everything's falling apart.

Dr. Elias: I hear you. And yet—what if none of it is wrong?

Maya: What?

Dr. Elias: What if what you're experiencing isn't wrong, but simply unfolding? What if, in the larger scheme, it's exactly as it needs to be?

Maya: That sounds like denial. Or delusion.

Dr. Elias: Actually, it's neurobiology; and quantum physics; and cognitive science. But more than that, it's remembering. Let me explain.

Scientific Insight: The Dot Theory

In 2005, Steve Jobs told Stanford graduates: "You can't connect the dots looking forward; you can only connect them looking backward." He was paraphrasing what researchers in retrospective coherence have found: our brains are wired to seek meaning after the fact. This is known as narrative hindsight bias—our cognitive tendency to make sense of past events by linking them into a coherent story (Roese & Vohs, 2012).

But what if we could live our lives from that wisdom? What if we could trust—not the dots—but the deeper intelligence behind them? That's what we call the Pre-Conditioned Self.

The Pre-Conditioned Self: A Layered Return

You came into this world with Clarity, Curiosity, Wonder, Playfulness, and Love. But life taught you fear. It taught you shame. It taught you to brace. And so, you forgot.

Our work isn't to become something new. Our work is to remember who we were before we were told we were not enough.

The Four Layers of Remembering

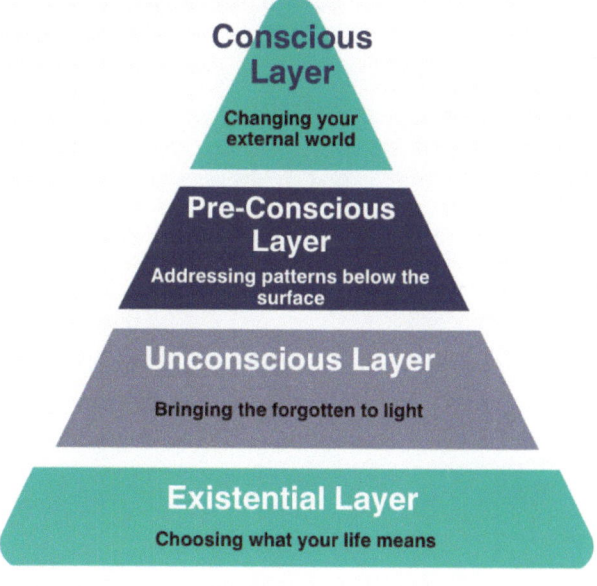

1. Conscious Layer – Behavior and Lifestyle

You start by changing your external world:
- Create structure.
- Practice mindfulness.
- Improve sleep, food, breath, movement, focus.
- Observe your thoughts (CBT).
- Practice box breathing, meditation, schedule optimization.

2. Preconscious Layer – Schema and Core Beliefs

Here, you address the patterns below the surface:
- What beliefs shape your reactions?
- What stories do you keep living out?
- Use Schema Therapy, ACT, Gestalt, and Mindfulness to rewire your map.

3. Unconscious Layer – Repressed Emotion and the Unseen

- Free associate.
- Analyze your dreams.
- Let the unconscious speak.
- Use psychoanalytic tools to bring the forgotten to light.

4. Existential Layer – Meaning, Freedom, Responsibility

- Choose what your life means.
- Embrace your freedom.
- Let go of "shoulds" and embrace "I choose."

Maya: So, you're saying all this suffering I've gone through—it wasn't random?

Dr. Elias: Not at all. In fact, in remembering, you'll see—it was your curriculum, your invitation, your training ground.

Maya: But I still feel pain.

Dr. Elias: Of course. But now you know—it's not what's happening that's causing the pain. It's how you're relating to it.

CBT Insight: The Thought-Emotion Link

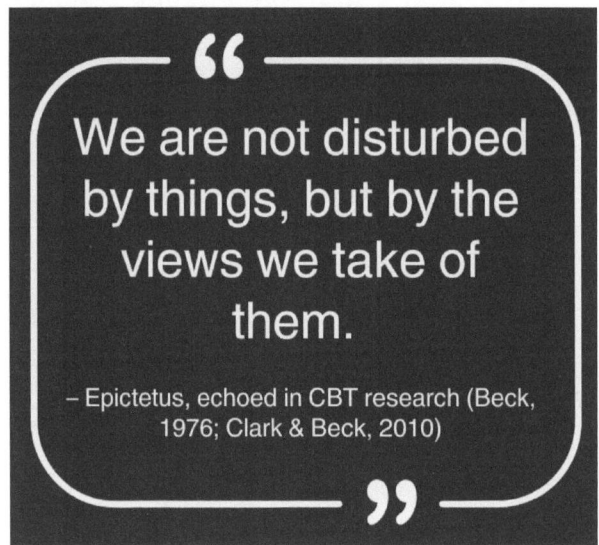

> We are not disturbed by things, but by the views we take of them.
>
> – Epictetus, echoed in CBT research (Beck, 1976; Clark & Beck, 2010)

Studies in cognitive behavioral therapy consistently show that thoughts mediate emotion and behavior. Change your interpretation, and you change your emotional response—even if the situation doesn't change (Hofmann et al., 2012).

Reflection Prompt:

Where in your life are you believing something is "wrong"? How would your experience change if you began with the premise: "This too is perfect"?

Implementation Tools:
- **Daily Remembering Practice**: Each morning, ask: What is perfect about today, even if I can't see it yet?
- **Reframe Journal**: Identify one negative thought per day and reframe it through the four layers.
- **Dot Connection Log**: Track three moments where things that felt like setbacks turned out to be blessings.

Commitment Statement:

"I commit to remembering that what I'm experiencing is not the problem—it's how I relate to it. I commit to trusting the dots."

Scientific References (Chapter 1):

- Beck, A.T. (1976). Cognitive Therapy and the Emotional Disorders.
- Hofmann, S. G., Asnaani, A., Vonk, I. J., Sawyer, A. T., & Fang, A. (2012). The Efficacy of Cognitive Behavioral Therapy: A Review of Meta-analyses. Cognitive Therapy and Research, 36(5), 427–440.
- Roese, N. J., & Vohs, K. D. (2012). Hindsight bias. Perspectives on Psychological Science, 7(5), 411–426.

Chapter 2: The Conditioned Self

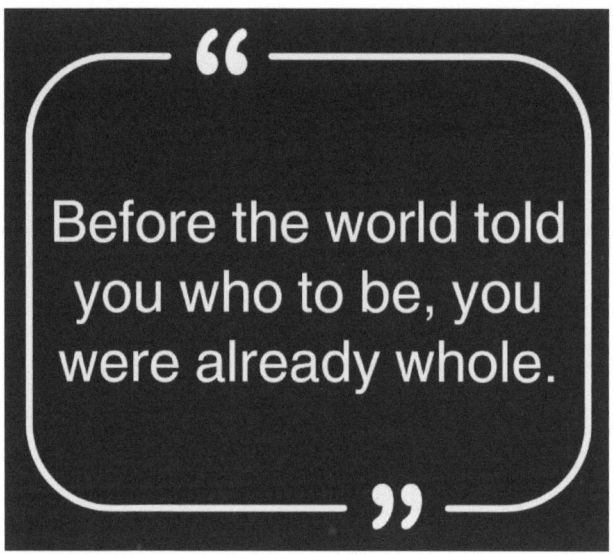

Maya: (reflecting on her recent visit to her childhood home) I felt like I was someone else there. Lighter. Braver. I don't know when I lost that version of me.

Dr. Elias: You didn't lose her. You buried her. Under layers of conditioning.

Maya: Conditioning?

Dr. Elias: Let's unpack it.

The Conditioned Self Defined
The Conditioned Self is not your authentic identity.
It is your survival identity—formed not by truth, but by adaptation.

It's the self that says:
- "Be quiet, or you'll get hurt."
- "Try harder, or you'll be left behind."
- "Don't cry, or you'll be seen as weak."

It's made up of every "should," "must," and "have to" you internalized to feel safe, accepted, or worthy.

And it is not your fault.

Scientific Insight: How Conditioning Happens

In developmental psychology, conditioning begins early—before language. Infants internalize emotional states from caregivers through limbic resonance (Lewis, Amini, & Lannon, 2000). As they grow, their behavior is shaped by operant conditioning (Skinner, 1953), attachment patterns (Bowlby, 1988), and social scripts (Berne, 1964).

Your brain literally wires itself to survive—through the formation of neural pathways that favor patterns of avoidance, performance, people-pleasing, or perfectionism (Siegel, 2012).

This becomes your identity. Not because it's true—but because it worked.

From Adaptation to Identification

What begins as a way to survive…
Becomes a way of being.

We forget it was once optional.

And so, we say:
- "I'm just an anxious person."
- "I've always been a fixer."
- "I can't help but people-please."
- "I'm not lovable unless I achieve."

But these are not you.
They are scripts.
And they are not your truth.

The Four Layers of Conditioning
1. Conscious Conditioning
The habits and behaviors we model after adults or authority figures.
- Tone of voice
- Productivity obsession
- External validation seeking
- Disconnection from body needs (sleep, rest, hunger)

2. Preconscious Conditioning
The beliefs we picked up without realizing:
- "I must be needed to be loved."
- "My worth is based on others' approval."
- "If I show emotion, I'll be abandoned."

These schemas run beneath awareness but dictate behavior.

3. Unconscious Conditioning
The deeply buried associations and traumas:
- Repressed shame
- Split-off parts of self
- Ancestral trauma and cultural messages

These are often accessed only through therapy, dreams, and deep emotional work.

4. Existential Conditioning
When society defines your value, purpose, and identity.
- What does it mean to be successful?
- Who gets to matter?
- What does a "good life" look like?

This is where the most dangerous lie lives: "You are not enough."

Dialogue Continued

Maya: So, all these years I've been chasing success, perfection, approval...I wasn't really choosing any of it?

Dr. Elias: You were surviving. But survival is not the same as living. And the minute we recognize the conditioned self, we're free to remember the truth.

Reflection Prompts
- What messages did you receive as a child about who you had to be?
- What were you rewarded for? Punished for?
- What do you believe you must do to be worthy?
- What have you internalized that may not be true?

Implementation Tools

Tool 1: Conditioning Awareness Worksheet
List three areas of your life where you feel stuck.
Then ask:
- What would my conditioned self say here?
- What would my preconditioned self know instead?

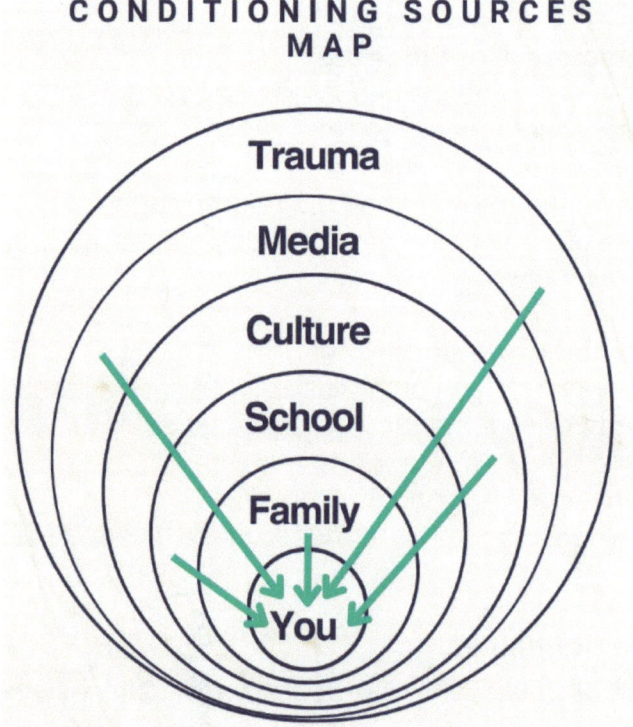

Tool 2: Inner Script Rewriting

Take a belief like, "I'm only valuable when I produce."
Now reframe it:
- Original belief: "My worth is tied to productivity."
- New belief: "I am worthy by being, not by doing."

Tool 3: Unmasking Meditation

Use breath awareness and visualization to imagine removing the "masks" of conditioning—one at a time. End with the self-affirming statement: I return to who I was before I was told who to be.

Commitment Statement

"I commit to recognizing the parts of me that were conditioned for survival—and I choose now to remember who I truly am."

Scientific References (Chapter 2):

- Bowlby, J. (1988). A Secure Base: Parent-Child Attachment and Healthy Human Development.
- Berne, E. (1964). Games People Play.
- Lewis, T., Amini, F., & Lannon, R. (2000). A General Theory of Love.
- Skinner, B. F. (1953). Science and Human Behavior.
- Siegel, D. J. (2012). The Developing Mind: How Relationships and the Brain Interact to Shape Who We Are.

Chapter 3: Why We Suffer

The Lens of Perception

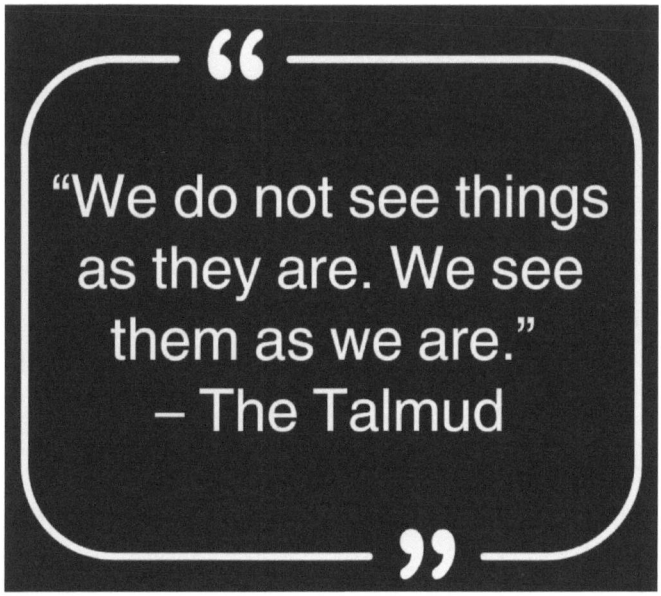

"We do not see things as they are. We see them as we are."
– The Talmud

Maya: You keep saying I can stop suffering. But how? My circumstances haven't changed. I still feel the weight.

Dr. Elias: It's not your circumstances that are causing your suffering, Maya. It's how you're relating to them. It's your perception—the lens you're looking through.

Maya: You're saying it's all in my head?

Dr. Elias: No. I'm saying it's all in your relationship to your head. Let's explore that.

Suffering vs. Pain

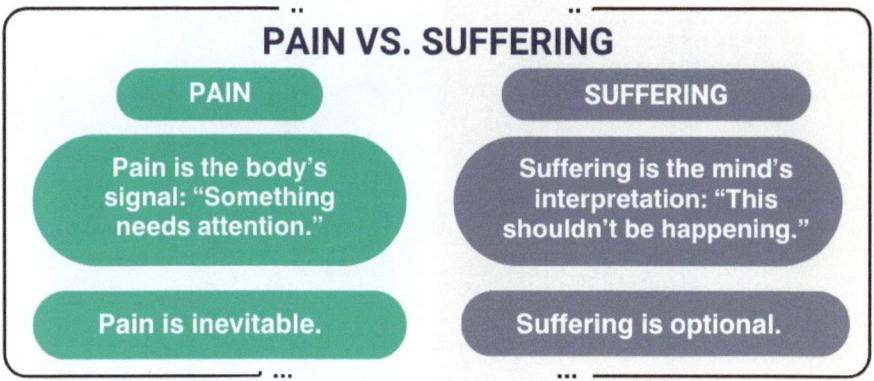

Pain is inevitable.
Suffering is optional.

Pain is the body's signal: "Something needs attention."
Suffering is the mind's interpretation: "This shouldn't be happening."

We suffer not because life is hard—but because we believe it shouldn't be.

We suffer because:
- We resist what is
- We cling to what was
- We fear what might be

Scientific Insight: Cognitive Appraisal Theory
According to Lazarus and Folkman's theory of cognitive appraisal (1984), our emotional response is not determined by the situation itself, but by how we interpret it. The same event—a breakup, a diagnosis, a rejection—can result in devastation or liberation, depending on meaning.

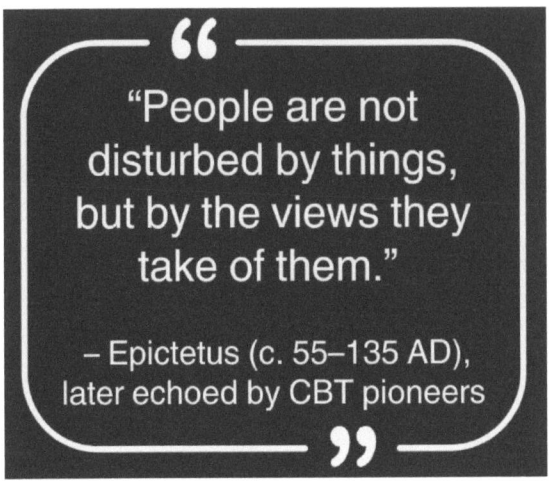

"People are not disturbed by things, but by the views they take of them."

– Epictetus (c. 55–135 AD), later echoed by CBT pioneers

The Four Layers of Suffering

Suffering compounds through layers. Transformation must therefore unfold layer by layer.

1. Conscious Layer – Resistance in Behavior
- Trying to fix, control, numb, avoid
- Overworking, overeating, overscheduling
- Tension in the body, shallow breathing

"I must escape this."

2. Preconscious Layer – Story and Interpretation
- "This means I'm a failure."
- "I'll never be okay again."
- "Bad things always happen to me."

These automatic beliefs shape emotional reactivity and behavior.

3. Unconscious Layer – Old Wounds and Patterns
- Pain echoes a past hurt you haven't healed
- You're not reacting to the present, but reliving the past
- Unconscious loyalty to suffering—because healing would mean facing the truth

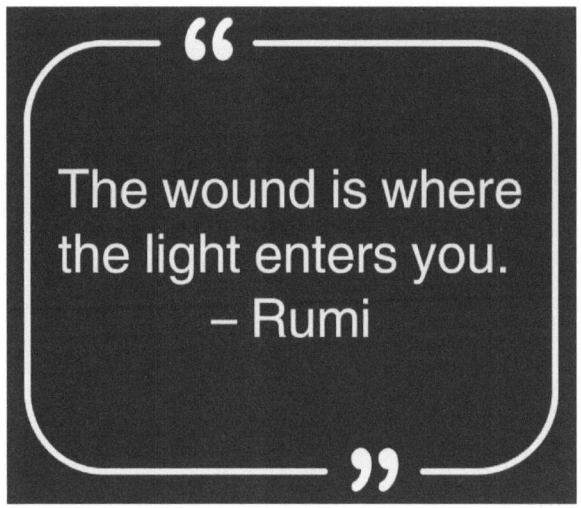

4. Existential Layer – Meaninglessness
- "What's the point?"
- "Why should I keep going?"
- "Life is suffering."

These beliefs stem from disconnection from meaning, purpose, and choice.

Maya: So, when I say, "I feel hopeless," what I'm really saying is...?

Dr. Elias: You're saying: "My thoughts feel hopeless." You're saying: "I'm interpreting this moment through a lens of despair." But you are not despair. You are the one watching the despair.

Reflection Prompts
- Where am I resisting what is?
- What story am I telling about my current challenge?
- Does this story come from now—or from then?
- If suffering is a lens, what would it feel like to take it off?

Implementation Tools
Tool 1: "What Else Could This Mean?" Exercise

Choose a recent moment of emotional distress.
Write your initial interpretation.
Now write three alternate interpretations.
Ask: Which one empowers me to grow?

Tool 2: Suffering Inventory

Write down:
- The event
- Your thoughts
- The feeling
- The belief behind it
    Then identify: Which layer is most active here—conscious, preconscious, unconscious, existential?

Tool 3: Radical Reality Acceptance Practice

Each morning, say aloud:

"This moment is not a mistake. I accept what is, even as I choose to grow."

Commitment Statement

"I commit to remembering that suffering arises not from life—but from my perception of it. I commit to changing the lens."

Maya: So, the situation might not change—but if my story does, the suffering dissolves?

Dr. Elias: Yes. You can be in pain… and still be at peace. You can hurt… and still feel free.

Scientific References (Chapter 3)

- Lazarus, R. S., & Folkman, S. (1984). Stress, Appraisal, and Coping.
- Beck, A. T. (1976). Cognitive Therapy and the Emotional Disorders.
- Hofmann, S. G., Asnaani, A., Vonk, I. J., Sawyer, A. T., & Fang, A. (2012). The Efficacy of Cognitive Behavioral Therapy: A Review of Meta-analyses.
- Linehan, M. M. (1993). Cognitive-Behavioral Treatment of Borderline Personality Disorder.
- Frankl, V. E. (1959). Man's Search for Meaning.

Chapter 4: The Myth of Control and the Fear of Uncertainty

Maya: (looking at her phone) I keep refreshing, checking, planning, re-planning. I just want to know how it's all going to turn out.

Dr. Elias: And what if not knowing is exactly where the healing begins?

Maya: That's terrifying.

Dr. Elias: Exactly. Most of our suffering doesn't come from life itself. It comes from our fight with uncertainty—our desperate need to control what was never ours to manage.

The Myth of Control
Control feels like safety.
But it's often a mask for fear.

We try to control:
- The outcome
- Others' opinions
- The timing
- The future

But control is a cognitive illusion—an attempt to override reality with our expectations.

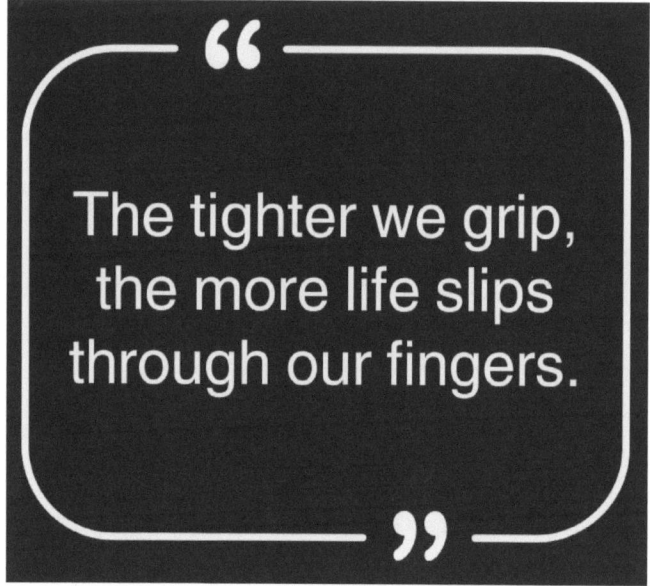

Scientific Insight: The Illusion of Control

In psychology, the illusion of control is a well-documented cognitive bias in which individuals overestimate their ability to influence outcomes that are objectively uncontrollable (Langer, 1975). This illusion temporarily reduces anxiety but reinforces avoidance of uncertainty tolerance.

Neuroscience studies show that intolerance of uncertainty activates the amygdala, the brain's threat detection system (Grupe & Nitschke, 2013). The more we resist uncertainty, the more chronically activated our stress response becomes.

The Four Layers of Control

Let's walk through how control shows up in each layer—and how to begin to heal.

1. Conscious Layer – Behavior and Environment
- Over-scheduling
- Re-checking
- Micromanaging
- Seeking constant reassurance

Behavioral goal: feel safe through predictability
Healing: Mindfulness, breathwork, flexibility practice, letting go rituals

2. Preconscious Layer – Beliefs and Schemas
- "If I don't do it, it won't get done."
- "If I plan enough, I can prevent bad things."
- "Uncertainty means danger."

These beliefs run silently and dictate behavior.

Healing: Schema Therapy, ACT (Acceptance and Commitment Therapy), reframing exercises

3. Unconscious Layer – Fear and Emotional Memory
- Childhood chaos, abandonment, or instability
- Past trauma that made uncertainty feel life-threatening
- Repressed grief or helplessness beneath the drive to control

Healing: Free association, somatic awareness, dream work, depth psychotherapy

4. Existential Layer – Meaning and Surrender
- "If I'm not in control, who am I?"
- "Does life care about me?"
- "What if I trust, and everything falls apart?"

These questions often surface only in moments of surrender.

Healing: Existential therapy, spiritual inquiry, meaning-making, radical trust

Dr. Elias: Control is a placeholder for trust. The more we try to manage the uncontrollable, the further we drift from remembering the truth: You were never meant to control it. You were meant to partner with it.

Reflection Prompts
- Where in your life are you gripping tightly?
- What are you afraid might happen if you let go?
- What early memory might be fueling your need for certainty?
- What would trust feel like, even without control?

Implementation Tools
Tool 1: The Letting Go Practice
At the start and end of each day, identify:
- One thing you're trying to control
- One action you can take (if any)
- One thing to surrender

Then repeat:
"I trust that life is unfolding in my favor, even when I can't see it."

Tool 2: Uncertainty Reframe Script
When you feel anxious, ask:
- What am I afraid of not knowing?
- What would I tell a friend in this same moment?
- Can I be with this feeling, even just for one breath?

Tool 3: Trust Muscle Exercise

Track one moment per day where you let go of something small and it turned out okay.
(Ex: Not checking your email late at night. Letting someone else lead. Trusting your body's rhythm.)

Small steps build your trust muscle—it's neuroplasticity at work.

Commitment Statement

"I commit to loosening my grip on what was never mine to control. I commit to building trust, one surrendered breath at a time."

Maya: So, the goal isn't to control less—it's to trust more?

Dr. Elias: Exactly. Control is exhausting. Trust is sustainable. And every moment of letting go… is a moment of remembering who you really are.

Scientific References (Chapter 4)

- Langer, E. J. (1975). The illusion of control. Journal of Personality and Social Psychology, 32(2), 311–328.
- Grupe, D. W., & Nitschke, J. B. (2013). Uncertainty and anticipation in anxiety: An integrated neurobiological and psychological perspective. Nature Reviews Neuroscience, 14(7), 488–501.
- Hayes, S. C., Strosahl, K. D., & Wilson, K. G. (1999). Acceptance and Commitment Therapy: An Experiential Approach to Behavior Change.
- Siegel, D. J. (2012). The Developing Mind: How Relationships and the Brain Interact to Shape Who We Are.

Chapter 5: The Architecture of the Mind

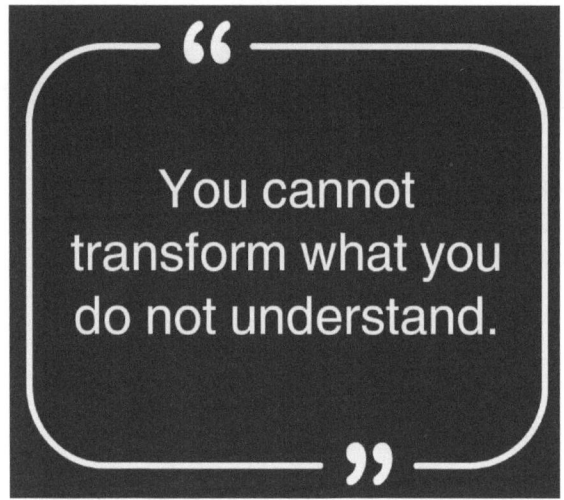

Maya: Why does it feel like I understand everything when I'm here with you—and then when I'm alone, I forget again?

Dr. Elias: Because remembering doesn't start in your mind. It starts in your structure.

Maya: What do you mean?

Dr. Elias: It's time I show you how your mind really works.

The Four Rooms of the Mind

Imagine your mind as a house. Most people only live in the living room—the conscious mind—but there are three other rooms. They're all running the show.

Let's go through them:

1. The Conscious Layer
This is the realm of logic, willpower, structure, and awareness.

It includes:
- Daily routines
- Habits
- Actions and behaviors
- Language and thought
- Executive function (e.g., planning, organizing)

This is where CBT and behavioral modification tools operate. But here's the truth: This layer is only about 5% of the mind's activity (Bargh & Morsella, 2008). It's the tip of the iceberg.

Maya: So, I'm trying to change my life from just 5% of my power?

Dr. Elias: Exactly. You're rowing a boat with one oar—and wondering why you're spinning in circles.

2. The Preconscious Layer
This is the bridge between the conscious and unconscious.

It includes:
- Core beliefs
- Internal schemas
- Early life narratives
- Attachment styles
- Subconscious emotional reactions

This layer is shaped by childhood, culture, trauma, and repetition. You can access it through journaling, mindfulness, schema therapy, or deep inquiry.

Scientific Insight:
Preconscious content is retrievable with effort and introspection. It shapes perception and judgment outside of awareness (Kihlstrom, 1987).

This is where Gestalt Therapy, Acceptance and Commitment Therapy (ACT), and Schema Therapy become powerful.

3. The Unconscious Layer

The deepest storage vault—home of:
- Repressed trauma
- Dreams
- Instincts
- Defense mechanisms
- Unresolved conflicts
- The shadow self

You can't access this layer by thinking harder.
You must feel, free associate, dream, explore.

This is the land of psychoanalysis—of Freud, Jung, and modern depth therapies.

Dr. Elias: Your unconscious is not your enemy. It's the part of you that tried to protect you when no one else did.

Maya: Even the parts I hate?

Dr. Elias: Especially those.

FREUD'S TOPOGRAPHICAL ICEBERG MODEL

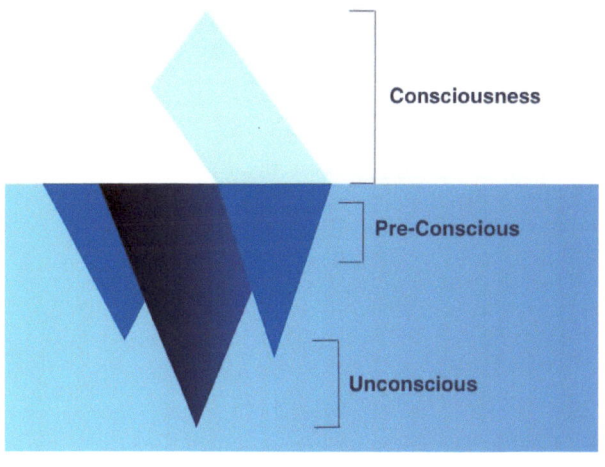

4. The Existential Layer

Beyond the personal.
Here lives your:
- Freedom
- Meaning
- Purpose
- Responsibility
- Spiritual identity
- Universal truth

This is the layer of transformation. The place where people stop asking, "Why me?" and start asking, "Why not me—and what do I do now?"

Here, we practice:
- Existential psychotherapy
- Logotherapy
- The Golden Rule
- Radical responsibility
- Forgiveness
- Spiritual integration

Integration: The Whole Mind, Whole Self

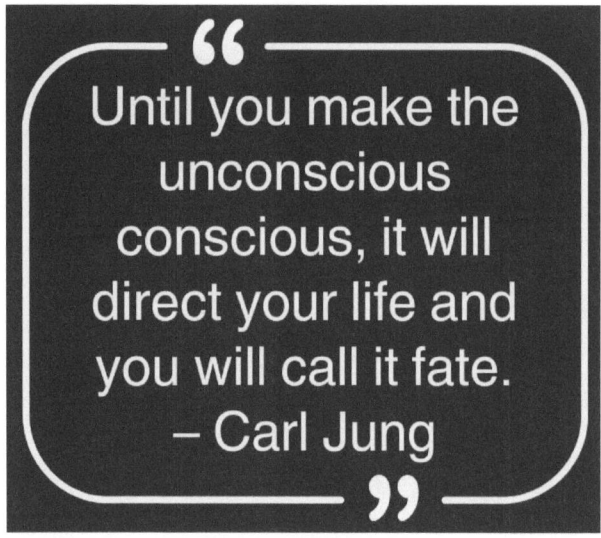

> "Until you make the unconscious conscious, it will direct your life and you will call it fate."
> – Carl Jung

You are not just your conscious thoughts.
You are a system of layers, longing to be remembered and re-united.

Reflection Prompt:
- Which layer do you spend most of your time in?
- Which layer have you avoided the most?
- What might be waiting for you in the layers below?

Implementation Tools:
- Layered Check-In: Morning journaling asking:
    1. What am I doing (Conscious)?
    2. What am I believing (Preconscious)?
    3. What might I be avoiding or repressing (Unconscious)?
    4. What am I choosing to live for today (Existential)?

- Mind Map Practice: Draw your "mind house" and identify real-life examples of what's in each layer.
- Therapy Audit: Review your current approach—are you working on all four layers?

Commitment Statement:

"I commit to honoring every layer of my mind, not just the part I can see. I commit to walking through every room of my inner house."

Scientific References (Chapter 5):

- Bargh, J. A., & Morsella, E. (2008). The unconscious mind. Perspectives on Psychological Science, 3(1), 73–79.
- Kihlstrom, J. F. (1987). The cognitive unconscious. Science, 237(4821), 1445–1452.
- Freud, S. (1915). The Unconscious. Standard Edition, Vol. 14.
- Jung, C.G. (1964). Man and His Symbols.
- Yalom, I.D. (1980). Existential Psychotherapy. Basic Books.

PART II: THE REMEMBERING

Chapter 6: The Preconditioned Self

Who You Were Before the World Told You Who to Be

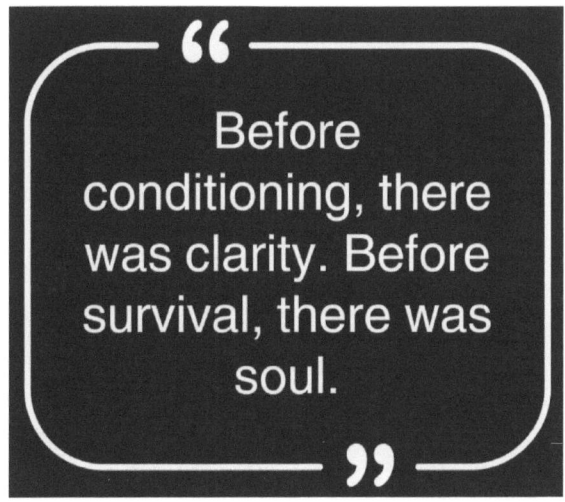

"Before conditioning, there was clarity. Before survival, there was soul."

Maya: So, if I'm not who I've been conditioned to be…Then who am I?

Dr. Elias: That, Maya, is the most important question you will ever ask. And the answer is simple, but not easy: You are who you were before the world interrupted.

The Preconditioned Self Defined

Your Preconditioned Self is your original design.
It is the unshaped you—the you that existed before fear, shame, conformity, and striving.

It is:
- Curious
- Creative
- Calm
- Present
- Connected
- Worthy—without needing to earn it

The Preconditioned Self is the truth before distortion.
It is the source—not the strategy.

Scientific Insight: Developmental Freedom

Before the age of two, children express a wide range of emotional and creative responses without inhibition. They live in what developmental theorists call the True Self (Winnicott, 1960)—a spontaneous, present-centered being state. This self is gradually obscured as children adapt to the demands of their caregivers and environment.

According to neuroscience, early attachment experiences shape the structure and function of the brain (Schore, 1994), creating neural pathways that favor conditioned safety over authentic expression. But—thanks to neuroplasticity—those pathways can be rewritten.

The Preconditioned Self isn't gone.
It's simply been covered—not erased.

The Four Layers of Returning to the Preconditioned Self

To return, we must move through the same layers that led us away.

1. Conscious Layer – Reconnecting Through Behavior
- Stillness practices
- Creative expression
- Nature immersion
- Play, dance, music, touch
- Breath awareness

These remind your body what it feels like to be home.

"The body remembers how to be free."

2. Preconscious Layer – Reclaiming Belief
- "I am worthy without proving."
- "Joy is my birthright."
- "I am already whole."

Repetition, journaling, and schema rewiring help replace old scripts with true beliefs.

3. Unconscious Layer – Meeting the Buried Self
- Dreams where you were wild, brave, or free
- Memories of childhood awe
- Fantasies you buried out of fear of ridicule

This is the level of deep reclaiming. The child you were is still inside—waiting to be remembered.

4. Existential Layer – Choosing to Live from Essence
- Letting go of roles, labels, and expectations
- Asking: What kind of human do I want to be?
- Embracing life not as a problem to solve but as a paradox to live

This is where you stop chasing and start being.

Maya: How do I know when I'm operating from that place?

Dr. Elias: You'll feel peaceful—even if the world isn't. You'll feel full—even if nothing gets accomplished. You'll feel like you—finally.

Reflection Prompts
- Who were you before you learned to be afraid?
- What did you love doing before someone told you it didn't matter?
- What qualities have you suppressed to "fit in"?
- When was the last time you felt completely yourself?

Implementation Tools
Tool 1: The Preconditioned Self Portrait

Draw or write a description of your truest self. Not who you've become—but who you are.
Include:
- Qualities
- Desires
- Values
- Feelings

Hang it where you can see it daily.

Tool 2: Remembering Ritual

Every morning, say aloud:

"I remember who I was before the world told me who to be. And I choose to return—today."

Use this as an anchor during moments of doubt.

Tool 3: Self-Inventory Across the 4 Layers
- Conscious: What am I doing that's integrated with my true self?
- Preconscious: What belief is supporting that?
- Unconscious: What fear or old pain is being challenged by it?
- Existential: How does this choice express who I really am?

Commitment Statement

"I commit to remembering the one I was before fear taught me to forget. I reclaim my Preconditioned Self as the foundation of my freedom."

Maya: So, remembering is not just an idea. It's a practice.

Dr. Elias: Exactly. You don't need to become someone new. You need to return to the one you were always meant to be.

Scientific References (Chapter 6)
- Winnicott, D. W. (1960). The Maturational Processes and the Facilitating Environment.
- Schore, A. N. (1994). Affect Regulation and the Origin of the Self.
- Siegel, D. J. (2012). The Developing Mind: How Relationships and the Brain Interact to Shape Who We Are.
- Porges, S. W. (2011). The Polyvagal Theory: Neurophysiological Foundations of Emotions, Attachment, Communication, and Self-regulation.
- Cozolino, L. (2010). The Neuroscience of Psychotherapy: Healing the Social Brain.

Chapter 7: Meaning, Memory, and the Inner Map

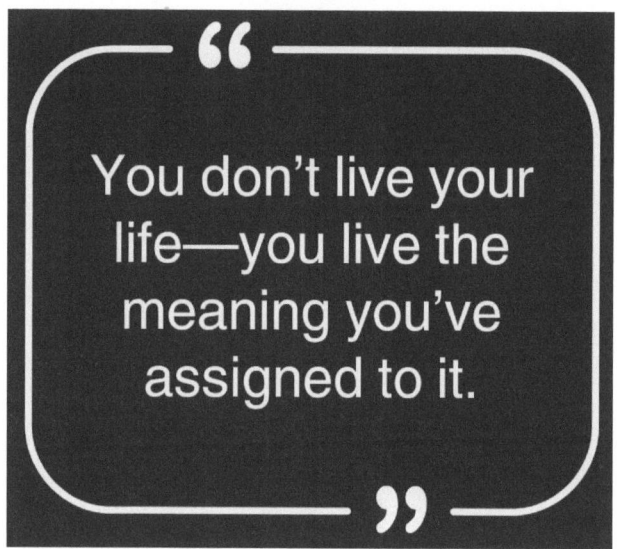

Maya: I've been thinking…Maybe I've been living out a story that was never mine.

Dr. Elias: Exactly. We don't suffer from the events of our lives— we suffer from the meaning we've given those events. And that meaning becomes our map.

The Inner Map
Your brain is a storyteller.
It doesn't just record events—it interprets them.

That interpretation becomes your inner map.
And that map determines:

- Where you go
- What you expect
- What you avoid
- Who you think you are

But here's the truth:
The map is not the territory.
It's just the version of reality your brain built to survive.

"The story you tell becomes the life you live."

Scientific Insight: Memory Is Not Objective

Neuroscience confirms: Memory is meaning-based, not fact-based.

According to research by Schacter (1999), memory is reconstructive, not reproductive. We remember what fits our schema—our emotional blueprint.

Trauma researchers like van der Kolk (2014) have shown that implicit memory (emotional and somatic memory) drives behavior without conscious awareness.

We act from a map built in childhood—one that may no longer serve us.

The Four Layers of Mapping and Meaning

To change our life, we don't need a better path.
We need a better map.

1. Conscious Layer – Thoughts and Stories

- "I'm always behind."
- "People can't be trusted."
- "Nothing ever works out."

  These surface beliefs dictate your actions.

Healing: CBT, self-affirming statements, journaling, thought reframing

2. Preconscious Layer – Schema and Emotional Memory
- Deep-seated narratives like:
    - "I'm invisible."
    - "Love is conditional."
    - "I must stay small to be safe."
- These patterns feel "normal" because they've always been there.

Healing: Schema therapy, mindfulness, ACT, guided inquiry

3. Unconscious Layer – Forgotten Wounds, Repetitions
- Repetitive relationship patterns
- Dream symbolism
- Emotional flashbacks without clear triggers
These are signs of unresolved meaning loops.

Healing: Dream work, psychoanalysis, parts work, EMDR

4. Existential Layer – Meaning, Purpose, and Narrative Identity
- Who do you believe you are?
- What is your life about?
- Are you the author—or just the reader—of your story?

Healing: Logotherapy, existential therapy, narrative re-authorship

Maya: So, I've been living based on a map I didn't even know I was following?

Dr. Elias: Yes. And the most powerful moment of your life is the moment you realize: You can rewrite the map.

Reflection Prompts
- What recurring emotional themes show up in your life?
- What story do you keep telling about who you are?
- What have you decided certain events meant about you?
- If you could rewrite the meaning, what would you say instead?

Implementation Tools

Tool 1: "Rewrite the Meaning" Exercise

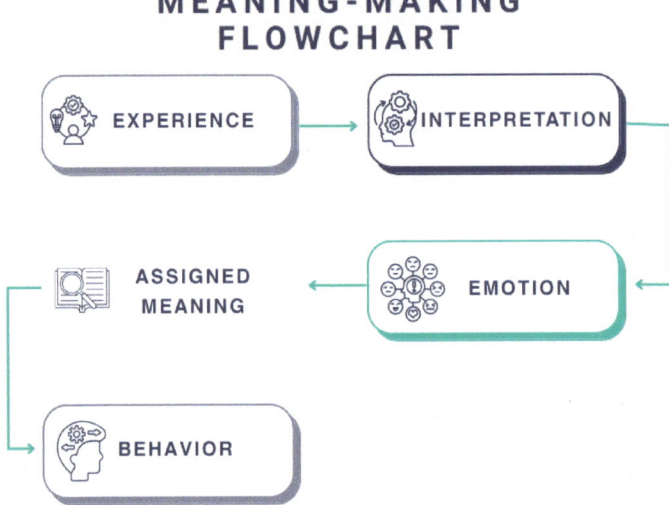

Identify a memory that still causes pain.
Then ask:
- What meaning did I assign to it at the time?
- Is that meaning still serving me?
- What new meaning would honor my growth?

End with this statement: "That happened. But I now decide what it means."

Tool 2: The Map Audit
Draw a map of your inner world:
- What are the "danger zones"?
- What paths do you avoid?
- What "landmarks" (core memories) define your direction?

Ask: Is this map taking me where I want to go?

Tool 3: Author Your Identity

Write a new narrative identity using the prompt:

"I am someone who…"
Complete the sentence 10 different ways—without using roles or titles.
(Ex: "I am someone who turns pain into peace.")

Commitment Statement

"I commit to becoming the author of my life, not just the actor. I reclaim the power to choose what my experiences mean."

Maya: So, rewriting the map doesn't erase the past.

Dr. Elias: No. It reclaims it. It transforms it from a trap into a tool. From a scar into a source of strength.

Scientific References (Chapter 7)

- Schacter, D. L. (1999). The seven sins of memory: Insights from psychology and cognitive neuroscience.
- van der Kolk, B. A. (2014). The Body Keeps the Score: Brain, Mind, and Body in the Healing of Trauma.
- Young, J. E., Klosko, J. S., & Weishaar, M. E. (2003). Schema Therapy: A Practitioner's Guide.
- Frankl, V. E. (1959). Man's Search for Meaning.
- White, M., & Epston, D. (1990). Narrative Means to Therapeutic Ends.

Chapter 8: The Four Layers of Transformation

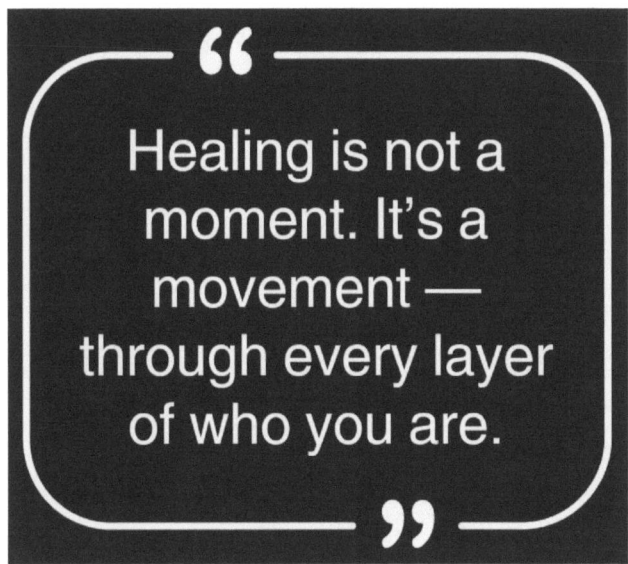

> Healing is not a moment. It's a movement — through every layer of who you are.

Maya: (reflecting on an outing with her friends to a sculpture garden) It was wild. I didn't even see what it really was until I moved around it.

Dr. Elias: That's transformation. You don't change the sculpture. You change the vantage point. And to do that, you have to move through all the layers.

What Is Transformation?

Transformation is not a single shift.
It's a layered remembering.

True, sustainable healing requires movement through four distinct — but interconnected — levels:

Conscious → Preconscious → Unconscious → Existential
Each layer has its own language.
Each requires its own tools.
And each must be honored for wholeness to emerge.

Scientific Insight: The Layered Brain

Your brain is layered, too.

- Conscious layer = Prefrontal cortex (executive function, planning)
- Preconscious = Limbic system (emotion, schema, memory)
- Unconscious = Brainstem & basal ganglia (autonomic survival patterns, implicit memory)
- Existential = Default mode network (self-concept, meaning-making)

Neuroplasticity allows change at every level—but each must be engaged differently (Cozolino, 2010; Porges, 2011).

The Four Layers of Transformation

LAYER HEALING MATRIX

LAYER	TOOLS
CONSCIOUS	• Letting go ritual • Reframe journaling • Daily breath awareness practice
PRECONSCIOUS	• Schema identification exercise • Values clarification • Belief challenge chart
UNCONSCIOUS	• Dream journal • Free association prompts • "What keeps repeating?" map
EXISTENTIAL	• Meaning inventory • "I am" identity statements • Golden Rule compass practice

1. The Conscious Layer – Structure and Behavior

What it includes:
- Habits, choices, schedules, actions
- Diet, sleep, movement, breath
- Thought awareness (CBT), mindfulness
- Time management, goal setting

Entry point:
Change what you do.

Modality examples:
- CBT, behavior activation, habit design, mindfulness

Tools from previous chapters:
- Letting go ritual
- Reframe journaling
- Daily breath awareness practice

2. The Preconscious Layer – Beliefs and Emotional Patterns

What it includes:
- Core beliefs
- Internal dialogue
- Schema and attachment patterns
- Automatic emotional responses

Entry point:
Observe what you believe and feel.

Modality examples:
- Schema therapy, ACT, Gestalt, mindfulness-based therapies

Tools:
- Schema identification exercise
- Values clarification
- Belief challenge chart

3. The Unconscious Layer – Repressed Memory and Wounds

What it includes:
- Forgotten pain
- Internalized trauma
- Dreams, slips, somatic clues
- Repetitive life patterns

Entry point:
Notice what keeps showing up that you haven't consciously chosen.

Modality examples:
- Psychoanalysis, EMDR, inner child work, somatic experiencing

Tools:
- Dream journal
- Free association prompts
- "What keeps repeating?" map

4. The Existential Layer – Meaning, Freedom, and Identity

What it includes:
- Self-definition
- Life philosophy
- Purpose and values
- Death awareness, spiritual orientation

Entry point:
Ask what your life is for.

Modality examples:
- Logotherapy, existential therapy, narrative therapy, spiritual inquiry

Tools:
- Meaning inventory
- "I am" identity statements
- Golden Rule compass practice

Dr. Elias: Most people try to heal at just one level. They journal, or meditate, or take medication, or go to therapy—but they stay in one room of the house.

Maya: And true transformation means walking through all the rooms?

Dr. Elias: Exactly. That's where the remembering lives.

Reflection Prompts
- Which layer have I focused on the most in my healing journey?
- Which layer have I avoided or not known how to approach?
- What's one next step I can take at each layer?

Implementation Tools

Tool 1: Layer Audit Journal

Create a four-column journal.
Each day, write:
- What did I do today that changed my behavior? (Conscious)
- What belief or emotional pattern surfaced? (Preconscious)
- What memory, dream, or repeating pattern showed up? (Unconscious)
- What meaning am I making of all of it? (Existential)

Tool 2: The 4-Layer Weekly Practice Plan

Create a weekly schedule with at least one intentional action per layer:
- Monday: Behavior shift
- Tuesday: Belief reframe
- Wednesday: Inner child dialogue or dream work
- Thursday: Reflect on meaning

This rotation allows integration over time.

Tool 3: Integration Circle Exercise

Draw four overlapping circles (Venn Diagram).
Label each: Conscious, Preconscious, Unconscious, Existential.
Add words, memories, tools, and practices that help you access each.
Look at the intersection.
That's your path forward.

Commitment Statement

"I commit to healing at every level of who I am. I commit to honoring each layer of transformation as sacred and necessary. I walk through the house of my soul—room by room—until I remember I am whole."

Maya: So, this is what it means to remember?

Dr. Elias: Yes. Not just to know. But to embody. Not just to heal the surface—but the source.

Scientific References (Chapter 8)

- Cozolino, L. (2010). The Neuroscience of Psychotherapy: Healing the Social Brain.
- Porges, S. W. (2011). The Polyvagal Theory.
- Beck, A. T. (1976). Cognitive Therapy and the Emotional Disorders.
- Young, J. E. et al. (2003). Schema Therapy: A Practitioner's Guide.
- Frankl, V. E. (1959). Man's Search for Meaning.
- Jung, C. G. (1964). Man and His Symbols.

Chapter 9: Thought Is Not Reality

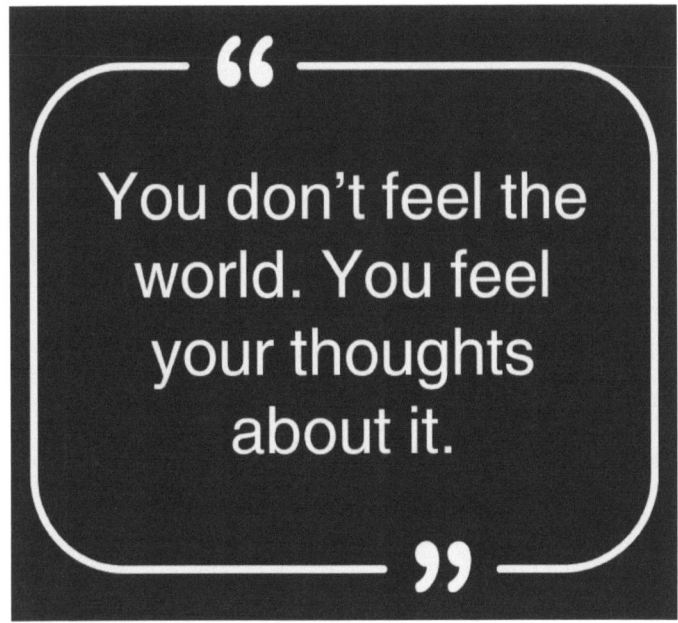

> "You don't feel the world. You feel your thoughts about it."

Maya: I realized something this morning. I woke up panicked. Nothing had even happened yet—but I already felt like I was failing the day.

Dr. Elias: That's not your life. That's your mind. And your mind—though brilliant—is not the truth. It's a narrator. Not a compass. A tool. Not a master.

The Fundamental Error: Equating Thought with Truth

Most of us confuse what we think with what is.

We say:
- "I'm unlovable."
- "This day is already ruined."
- "They must hate me."

And we act as though these thoughts are facts.

But thought is not reality.
Thought is a representation of reality—a mental construction based on past memory, internal schema, and emotional filters.

"You don't feel your life. You feel your thoughts about your life."

Scientific Insight: Cognitive Distortions and the Thinking Trap

Cognitive Behavioral Therapy (CBT) identifies common thinking errors—mental distortions that warp perception (Beck, 1976; Burns, 1980):

- Catastrophizing
- Mind reading
- All-or-nothing thinking
- Emotional reasoning

Neuroscience confirms that rumination and negative self-talk activate the brain's default mode network (DMN), increasing cortisol and anxiety (Zhang & Raichle, 2010).

The more we fuse with our thoughts, the more our emotional brain takes over.

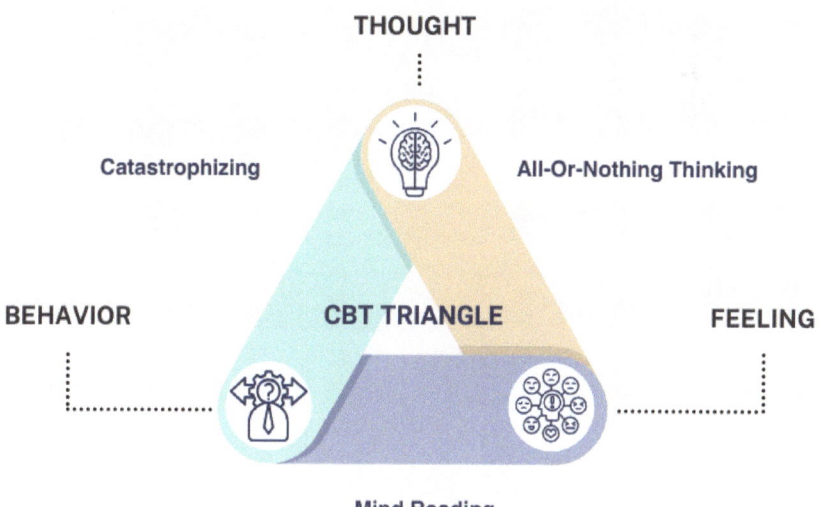

The Four Layers of Thought Distortion and Healing

1. Conscious Layer – Thought Awareness and Disruption

Symptoms:
- Racing thoughts
- Negative self-talk
- "Should" statements
- Rumination

Healing Tools:
- CBT thought record
- Mindfulness meditation
- Reframe exercises
- Journaling

Action: Write it. Name it. Reframe it.

2. Preconscious Layer – Beliefs Beneath the Thoughts

Symptoms:
- Repetitive thinking patterns
- Deep-seated themes (rejection, unworthiness)
- "I always mess things up" even after successes

Healing Tools:
- Schema identification
- Core belief replacement
- Compassion-based inquiry

Action: Ask: Where did this belief begin? Who taught it to me?

3. Unconscious Layer – Thought as Defense

Symptoms:
- Chronic overthinking to avoid feeling
- Intellectualizing trauma
- Dream themes involving chaos, judgment, or silence

Healing Tools:
- Free association
- Dream analysis
- Parts work or inner child exploration

Action: Notice what thoughts protect you from feeling.

4. Existential Layer – Identity and Meaning

Symptoms:
- "I am my thoughts."
- Life is defined by negative interpretations
- Lack of agency or spiritual orientation

Healing Tools:
- Defusion practices (ACT)
- Spiritual inquiry
- Values-based living

Action: Ask: If I'm not my thoughts, who am I really?

Maya: So, every time I think something painful, I don't have to believe it?

Dr. Elias: No. You can watch it float by. Like clouds across a sky, you never stop being.

Reflection Prompts
- What thought have I been treating as truth this week?
- What emotion is that thought creating?
- Who might I be without that thought?
- What would it look like to observe my thoughts instead of obeying them?

Implementation Tools
Tool 1: Thought Detective Worksheet
Each time you feel distress, ask:
1. What just happened?
2. What did I think about it?
3. Is it true?

4. Is it the only truth?
5. What else might be true?

Tool 2: Daily Defusion Practice

3 times per day, write a persistent negative thought.
Then say:

"I'm noticing that I'm having the thought that…"

Example:

"I'm noticing that I'm having the thought that I'm not doing enough."

Repeat 3x. Notice the shift in distance.

Tool 3: The Witness Meditation

Close your eyes.
Picture your thoughts as clouds or a river.
Let them pass.
Do not follow them—just watch.

End with:

"I am the sky. Not the storm."

Commitment Statement

"I commit to seeing my thoughts as thoughts—not facts. I choose to become the witness, not the prisoner, of my mind."

Maya: I don't have to change every thought. I just have to stop giving them power.

Dr. Elias: Exactly. Freedom doesn't begin with silence. It begins with space.

Scientific References (Chapter 9)
- Beck, A. T. (1976). Cognitive Therapy and the Emotional Disorders.
- Burns, D. D. (1980). Feeling Good: The New Mood Therapy.
- Hayes, S. C., Strosahl, K. D., & Wilson, K. G. (1999). Acceptance and Commitment Therapy.
- Zhang, D., & Raichle, M. E. (2010). The default mode network and self-referential processes in depression. Nature Reviews Neuroscience.
- Linehan, M. M. (1993). Cognitive-Behavioral Treatment of Borderline Personality Disorder.

Chapter 10: Living from the Inside-Out

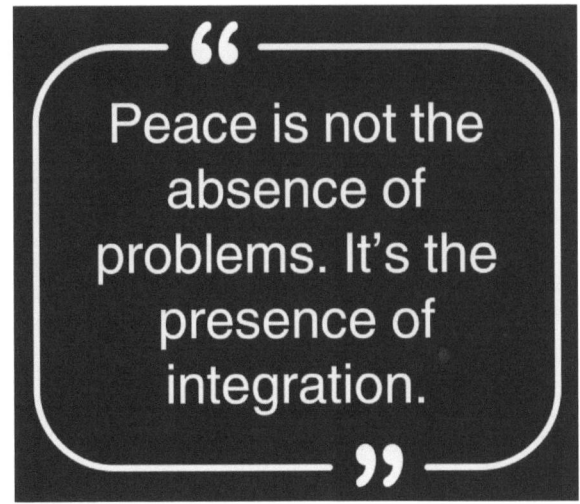

> "Peace is not the absence of problems. It's the presence of integration."

Maya: For the first time… I didn't check my phone when I woke up. I just breathed. Sat there.
And something inside me said, "This is it."

Dr. Elias: Yes. That's what it feels like to live from the inside-out. To be guided not by fear, approval, or performance—but by presence. By peace. By your truth.

The Outside-In World

Most of us are taught to live from the outside-in:
- What will they think?
- What do I need to do to be accepted?
- What if I fail?

This conditioning creates:
- Anxiety
- Burnout
- Disconnection from self
- Chronic comparison
- A life that looks good—but doesn't feel good

But there's another way.

The Inside-Out Paradigm

Living from the inside-out means:
- Your identity is not up for negotiation
- Your peace is not conditional
- Your compass is internal
- Your life is a response to your values, not a reaction to external chaos

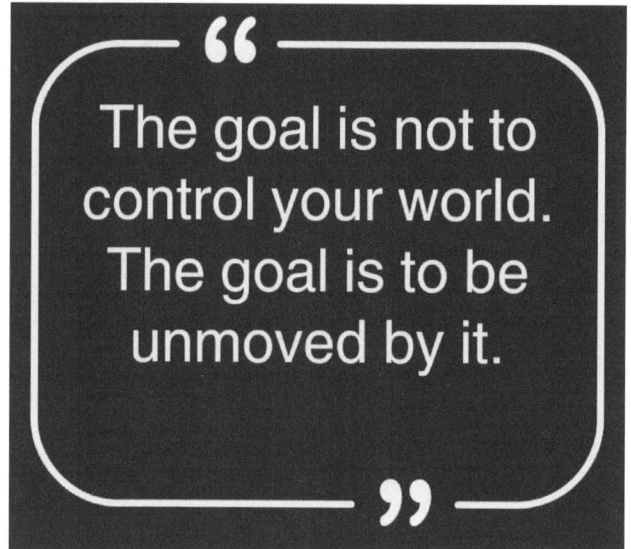

> "The goal is not to control your world. The goal is to be unmoved by it."

Scientific Insight: Internal Locus of Control and Eudaimonic Living

People who operate from an internal locus of control (Rotter, 1966) believe they shape their life through their own values and actions—not external approval or fate. This is linked to:
- Higher well-being
- Lower anxiety and depression
- Greater resilience

Psychologist Martin Seligman (2002) distinguishes hedonic happiness (based on outcomes) from eudaimonic well-being—a deep, sustainable form of fulfillment based on meaning, autonomy, and inner integration.

The Four Layers of Inside-Out Living

1. Conscious Layer – Action from Integration

Symptoms of outside-in living:
- Overcommitting
- Saying yes when you mean no
- Performing instead of participating

Shifts:
- Practice boundaries
- Schedule based on values
- Choose presence over perfection

Modality Tools:
- Time blocking based on core values
- Mindful decision-making

2. Preconscious Layer – Beliefs That Empower

Symptoms:
- "I must earn love."
- "I need validation to feel worthy."
- "If I rest, I'm lazy."

Shifts:
- "I am the source."
- "I choose based on my truth."
- "Rest is productive when integrated."

Modality Tools:
- ACT defusion
- Schema restructuring
- Core value clarification

3. Unconscious Layer – Inner Liberation

Symptoms:
- Unexplained dread in stillness
- Guilt when not over-performing
- Fear of disappointing others without knowing why

Shifts:
- Releasing inherited patterns
- Befriending inner child
- Creating safety in being, not doing

Modality Tools:
- Inner child meditation
- Free association: "What happens when I stop trying?"
- Dream tracking

4. Existential Layer – Identity, Integrity, and Inner Authority

Symptoms:
- Lost sense of self
- Looking to others to define what's meaningful
- Confusing success with significance

Shifts:
- "I define who I am."
- "My life is an offering."
- "Peace is my baseline."

Modality Tools:
- Logotherapy
- Spiritual inquiry
- Narrative identity writing

Maya: So, this isn't about fixing anything. It's about returning to what was always there.

Dr. Elias: Yes. Inside-out living doesn't add to you. It reveals you.

Reflection Prompts
- Where in my life am I performing instead of integrating?
- What external voices have I mistaken for my own?
- What does peace feel like in my body?
- If I trusted my inner compass, what decision would I make today?

Implementation Tools

Tool 1: Inner Compass Journal (Daily Prompt)

Each morning, ask:
1. What do I feel?
2. What do I need?
3. What do I value today?
4. What one action honors this?

End with:

"I live from the inside out."

Tool 2: The Integration Audit

Pick one area of life: work, relationships, health.
Ask:
- Am I doing this out of fear, obligation, or truth?
- What would inside-out living look like here?

Create one shift based on integration — not expectation.

Tool 3: Stillness Challenge

Spend 5 minutes daily with no task, no distraction.
Just be.
Track:
- What arises
- What your thoughts say
- What you remember about who you are

Commitment Statement

"I commit to living a life that reflects my truth — not just my training. I choose to be led by my inner compass. From this day forward, I live from the inside-out."

Maya: I don't need to wait for the world to change before I feel peace.

Dr. Elias: No. You change your world the moment you realize: It begins within.

Scientific References (Chapter 10)
- Rotter, J. B. (1966). Generalized expectancies for internal versus external control of reinforcement.
- Seligman, M. E. P. (2002). Authentic Happiness: Using the New Positive Psychology.
- Ryan, R. M., & Deci, E. L. (2001). On happiness and human potentials: A review of research on hedonic and eudaimonic well-being.
- Frankl, V. E. (1959). Man's Search for Meaning.
- Brown, B. (2010). The Gifts of Imperfection.

PART III: THE RETURN

Chapter 11: Radical Acceptance and the Gift of Suffering

> "What you resist imprisons you. What you accept transforms you."

Maya: *I used to think healing was about making the pain go away. Now I wonder if it's about making peace with the pain.*

Dr. Elias: *That's the turning point. Suffering is not a mistake. It's a doorway.*

The Illusion of Escape
We are taught to run from suffering.
To numb it. Fix it. Repress it.
But in that running, we get stuck.

Suffering says:
- "Something here wants to be seen."
- "Something here is ready to be transformed."

And the only way through… is through.

What Is Radical Acceptance?

Radical Acceptance means:
- Acknowledging what is—without resistance
- Letting go of the need to change, fix, or control the moment
- Choosing to be with pain, instead of arguing with it

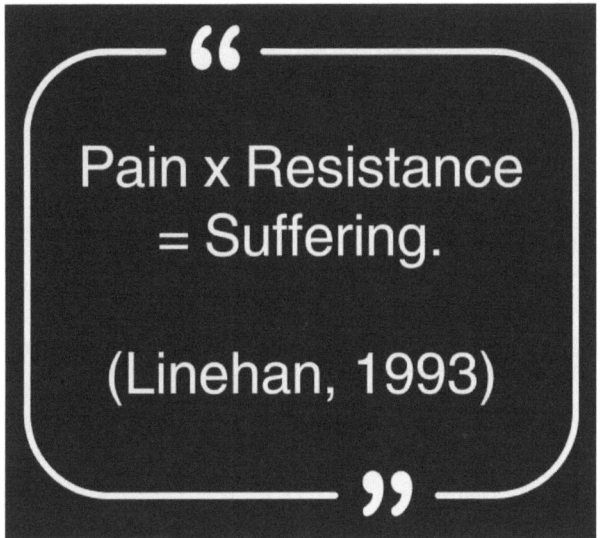

When you accept what is, you reclaim your power to choose what's next.

Scientific Insight: Acceptance and Psychological Flexibility

Acceptance is a core process in Acceptance and Commitment Therapy (ACT).

Research shows that individuals with greater psychological flexibility—the ability to stay present and open in the face of difficult emotions—experience:
- Less anxiety and depression
- More resilience
- Greater life satisfaction (Hayes et al., 2006)

Neuroimaging studies reveal that resisting emotion increases amygdala activity, while allowing emotion activates the prefrontal cortex—enhancing regulation and insight (Kober et al., 2010).

The Four Layers of Suffering—and Its Gifts

When we stop avoiding pain, we begin to understand it.
And from that understanding… comes wisdom.

1. Conscious Layer – Accepting What Is

Symptoms:
- Tight shoulders
- Sleepless nights
- Urgency to "solve" the pain

Shift:
- "This is what's happening. I don't have to like it, but I can allow it."

Tools:
- Mindfulness
- Breathwork
- Body scan
- Naming the emotion

2. Preconscious Layer – Accepting the Pattern

Symptoms:
- "Why does this always happen to me?"
- Guilt or shame around emotional reactions

Shift:
- "This pattern is trying to teach me something."

Tools:
- Pattern tracking
- Self-compassion
- Schema journaling

3. Unconscious Layer – Accepting the Wound

Symptoms:
- Emotional flashbacks
- Dreams or triggers
- Deep avoidance

Shift:
- "This pain is ancient. And it's ready to be seen."

Tools:
- Free writing
- Dream analysis
- Inner child work
- Psychoanalytic exploration

4. Existential Layer – Accepting the Invitation

Symptoms:
- "What's the point?"
- Grief without a name
- Identity crisis

Shift:
- "This is not punishment. This is passage."
- "This suffering is asking me to remember who I am."

Tools:
- Meaning-making
- Logotherapy
- Spiritual inquiry
- Gratitude for growth

Maya: So, pain isn't a failure…It's a portal.

Dr. Elias: Yes. Radical acceptance doesn't end suffering—it transforms it. It turns the wound into wisdom. The crack into light.

Reflection Prompts
- What am I still resisting in my life?
- What might this pain be here to teach me?
- What happens when I stop fighting what is?
- If this pain were a teacher, what would it say?

Implementation Tools
Tool 1: The R.A.I.N. Practice (Mindful Acceptance)
1. R – Recognize what is happening
2. A – Allow the experience to be there
3. I – Investigate with kindness
4. N – Nurture yourself with compassion

Practice daily, even for 5 minutes.

R.A.I.N. Process Map

Step	Description	Example
R – Recognize	Acknowledge what's happening inside you without judgment.	"I feel tight in my chest. I'm anxious."
A – Allow	Let the emotion, thought, or sensation be there without pushing it away.	"It's okay that I feel this. I don't have to fix it right now."
I – Investigate	Gently explore what the emotion is trying to tell you or where it's coming from.	"What's this anxiety about? Oh —it started after that email."
N – Nurture	Offer compassion, care, or wisdom to yourself. Speak to yourself like a friend.	"It's okay, love. You're doing your best. You don't have to be perfect."

Tool 2: The Suffering-to-Gift Journal

Pick a painful experience.
Ask:
- What was the suffering?
- What did I learn?
- Who have I become because of this?

Look for the gold in the ashes.

Tool 3: Acceptance Guiding Principle Meditation

Sit quietly and breathe.
Repeat:

"I allow what is. I accept this moment. I choose to trust the path I cannot yet see."

Let the guiding principle settle into your nervous system.

Commitment Statement

"I commit to no longer resisting what is. I open my heart to the wisdom inside my pain. I allow suffering to become my teacher."

Maya: So, the goal isn't to avoid suffering…It's to meet it with enough presence that it becomes something else.

Dr. Elias: Exactly. Suffering + Presence = Transformation. And the one who walks through it, is never the same.

Scientific References (Chapter 11)

- Linehan, M. M. (1993). Cognitive-Behavioral Treatment of Borderline Personality Disorder.
- Hayes, S. C., Strosahl, K. D., & Wilson, K. G. (2006). Acceptance and Commitment Therapy.
- Kober, H. et al. (2010). Prefrontal-striatal pathway underlies cognitive regulation of craving. PNAS.
- Neff, K. D. (2003). Self-compassion: An alternative conceptualization of a healthy attitude toward oneself.
- Frankl, V. E. (1959). Man's Search for Meaning.

Chapter 12: From Behavior to Belief

The Pathway to Freedom

"Every action teaches your brain what to believe. Every belief shapes how you act. This is the loop of identity—and it can imprison or liberate you."

Maya: I used to think I needed to believe something before I could act on it. But lately, I've noticed that when I act as if... something shifts.

Dr. Elias: That's the key. Belief doesn't always precede behavior. Sometimes, behavior births belief. And together, they shape identity.

The Behavior–Belief Loop
You act based on what you believe.
But what you do also reinforces what you believe.

This creates a feedback loop:

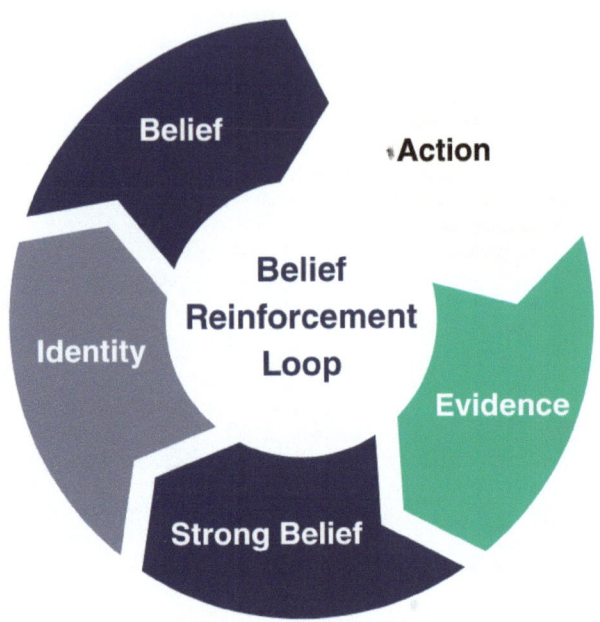

This loop is either:
- Empowering ("I can do hard things." → Take risk → Succeed → Believe in self), or
- Limiting ("I'm not good enough." → Avoid challenge → Stay stuck → Reinforce belief)

Scientific Insight: Behavior Shaping Belief

Cognitive dissonance theory (Festinger, 1957) shows that when our behavior contradicts our beliefs, the brain adapts—by changing the belief. This is why behavioral activation is a core component in treating depression: acting as if you're motivated leads to actual motivation (Jacobson et al., 2001).

Identity-based habits (Clear, 2018) also reinforce that small consistent actions reshape self-perception. You become the kind of person who meditates. The kind of person who speaks kindly. The kind of person who heals.

The Four Layers of the Behavior–Belief Pathway

Transformation is not just insight. It's practice. And practice is most powerful when applied at every level.

1. Conscious Layer – Habits Create Evidence

Symptoms:
- Inconsistent action
- Good intentions without follow-through
- Motivation that fades

Healing Focus:
- Build systems, not just willpower
- Act before you feel ready

Tools:
- Habit stacking
- Weekly accountability
- Implementation intentions ("If ___, then I will ___")

2. Preconscious Layer – Behavior Challenges Belief

Symptoms:
- "This isn't who I am."
- "I'm faking it."
- Internal conflict when trying something new

Healing Focus:
- Let actions teach your nervous system a new story
- Use exposure to self-efficacy

Tools:
- "As If" journaling
- Schema mapping + counter-behavior
- Positive evidence log ("I did it—even when…")

3. Unconscious Layer – Repetitions Reveal Wounds

Symptoms:
- Sabotaging success
- Avoidance of growth
- "I don't deserve this" reactions

Healing Focus:
- See the part of you afraid of new belief
- Integrate repressed fear or shame

Tools:
- Shadow work journaling: "What part of me fears being free?"
- Dream dialogue
- Guided reparenting meditations

4. Existential Layer – Choosing Identity Over Habit

Symptoms:
- Dependence on routine to feel "okay"
- Success without fulfillment
- Fragmentation between what you do and who you want to be

Healing Focus:
- Act based on who you choose to be
- Let actions express meaning

Tools:
- Identity affirmation: "I am someone who…"
- Purpose filter: "Does this serve the life I want to create?"
- Golden Rule compass: "Would I want this done to me?"

Maya: So, freedom isn't just about changing what I do…It's about changing why I do it—and what I let it teach me.

Dr. Elias: Exactly. Freedom is when action and belief flow from the same truth. When you stop betraying yourself. When you become a living expression of your values.

Reflection Prompts
- What do my current behaviors teach my brain to believe?
- Where do I say one thing—but do another?
- What identity do I want to embody through action?
- Where am I ready to act as if—until the belief catches up?

Implementation Tools

Tool 1: Behavior-Belief Integration Audit

List five regular behaviors. For each one, ask:
- What belief does this behavior reinforce?
- Is that the belief I want to live by?

Change one behavior to align with your chosen belief.

Tool 2: Identity-Based Habit Design

Complete this statement:

"I am someone who _____. Therefore, today I will _____."

Ex:

"I am someone who values peace. Therefore, today I will turn off my phone for one hour."

Track consistency—not perfection.

Tool 3: The Belief Bridge Practice

Pick a limiting belief (e.g., "I'm not confident").
Choose a bridge thought:

"I'm learning to feel confident."

Then take one small action that supports this bridge.

Repeat daily.

Commitment Statement

"I commit to integrating my actions with my deepest values. I choose behaviors that reflect who I'm becoming. I let my life become a mirror of the beliefs I choose."

Maya: This is how it happens, isn't it? Not all at once—but one integrated action at a time.

Dr. Elias: Yes. That's how we rewrite the script. That's how we step into freedom. By becoming who we are—through what we do.

Scientific References (Chapter 12)
- Festinger, L. (1957). A Theory of Cognitive Dissonance.
- Jacobson, N. S. et al. (2001). Behavioral Activation Treatment for Depression.
- Clear, J. (2018). Atomic Habits.
- Hayes, S. C., Strosahl, K. D., & Wilson, K. G. (1999). Acceptance and Commitment Therapy.
- Neff, K. D. (2011). Self-Compassion: The Proven Power of Being Kind to Yourself.

Chapter 13: Free Association and the Wisdom of the Unconscious

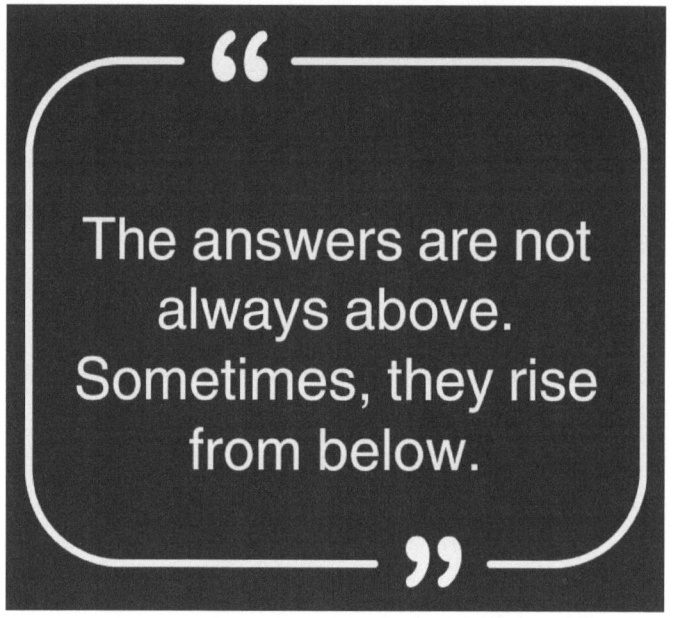

Maya: (reflecting on a journaling assignment) What if I don't know what to write? What if nothing comes?

Dr. Elias: That's the first defense. The unconscious speaks softly at first. But it will speak—if you stop trying to control the conversation.

Why the Unconscious Matters

The unconscious is not your enemy.
It is your archive.
It holds what you forgot. What you weren't ready to face. What you were told not to feel.

And it is full of wisdom.

What Is Free Association?

Free association is the practice of expressing thoughts, images, feelings, and memories as they arise—without censorship or structure.

It bypasses the logical, edited mind and gives voice to what's buried.

Freud called it the "royal road to the unconscious."
In modern terms, it is a direct access point to emotional truth, self-awareness, and inner freedom.

Scientific Insight: The Unconscious in Action

Modern neuroscience supports Freud's insight: much of what drives human behavior is unconscious.

- Implicit memory, unconscious bias, somatic triggers—all shape perception and choice before we are even aware of them (LeDoux, 2002; Siegel, 2012).
- Default mode network activity (associated with daydreaming, reflection, and internal narrative) increases during unstructured, non-goal-oriented thought—precisely the space that free association opens up (Andrews-Hanna et al., 2014).

The Four Layers of Unconscious Wisdom

Free association allows us to access, interpret, and integrate these four domains of the unconscious.

1. Conscious Layer – Opening the Gate

Symptoms of resistance:
- "I don't know what to say."
- "This is silly."
- Overthinking or controlling the process

Practice:
- Write or speak whatever arises, even if it's: "I don't know what to say."

Goal:
Build the habit of allowing. Lower the filter.

2. Preconscious Layer – Emerging Beliefs and Patterns

What appears:
- Themes, word repetitions
- Emotional imagery
- Hidden self-talk

Practice:
- Pause and reflect: "Where have I seen this before?"
- Ask: "What feeling is trying to surface?"

Modality tie-ins:
- Schema therapy, mindfulness, guided inquiry

3. Unconscious Layer – Forgotten or Repressed Content

What emerges:
- Vivid or symbolic imagery
- Early memories
- Somatic sensations
- "Accidental" words or slips

Practice:
- Free write for 20 minutes
- Circle emotionally charged words
- Use them to start another round

Modality tie-ins:
- Psychoanalysis, inner child work, parts work

4. Existential Layer – The Deep Voice Within

What surfaces:
- Questions of meaning, mortality, purpose
- Longing for something unnamed
- The voice of the soul

Practice:
- Ask: "What is this trying to awaken in me?"
- Let the unconscious speak not just of the past, but of the possibility for transformation

Maya: I thought healing was about understanding. But this… it feels like remembering.

Dr. Elias: Because it is. Your unconscious remembers who you were before fear began editing the story.

Reflection Prompts
- What am I afraid I might uncover if I stop censoring myself?
- What recurring symbols, dreams, or phrases show up in my life?
- What memories make me uncomfortable—even though I've "moved on"?
- What part of me has never had a voice?

Implementation Tools
Tool 1: Daily Free Association Practice
How to begin:
1. Set a timer for 10–20 minutes
2. Choose a starting phrase:
    - "Right now, I feel…"
    - "If I could speak without consequence…"
    - "The part of me that's silent says…"
3. Don't stop writing. Don't edit. Don't judge.

Tool 2: Post-Writing Review
After free association, use these questions:
- What surprised me?
- What themes or metaphors appeared?
- What might this be pointing to beneath the surface?

Tool 3: The Dream Dialogue
1. Write down your most recent dream
2. Let each character or image speak in first person
   - "I am the locked door…"
   - "I am the crashing wave…"
3. Ask: What is the emotional message here?

Commitment Statement

"I commit to allowing the wisdom I once buried to rise again. I give voice to the forgotten. I make room for the paradox. I remember what I've hidden—even from myself."

Maya: It's strange. The more I stop trying to control the process… The more I begin to trust what I find.

Dr. Elias: That's the gift of the unconscious. It's not trying to sabotage you. It's trying to return you to yourself.

Scientific References (Chapter 13)
- Freud, S. (1900). The Interpretation of Dreams.
- LeDoux, J. E. (2002). Synaptic Self: How Our Brains Become Who We Are.
- Siegel, D. J. (2012). The Developing Mind.
- Andrews-Hanna, J. R., et al. (2014). The brain's default network and its adaptive role in internal mentation.
- Jung, C. G. (1964). Man and His Symbols.

Chapter 14: The Existential Compass

Freedom, Meaning, and Choice

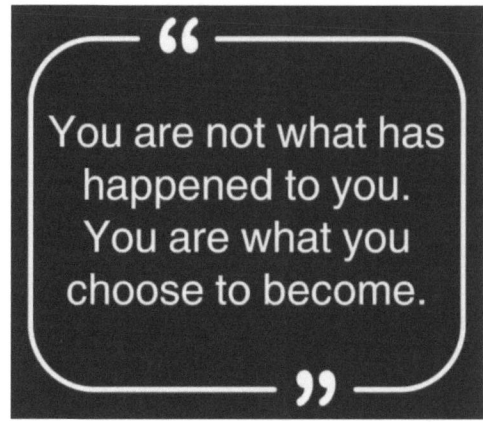

You are not what has happened to you. You are what you choose to become.

Maya: Everything up until now… I see it differently. I'm not just here to heal. I'm here to live—on purpose.

Dr. Elias: That's the existential shift. Healing is not the end. It's the beginning of living with freedom, meaning, and responsibility.

What Is the Existential Compass?

The Existential Compass is your inner orientation system.

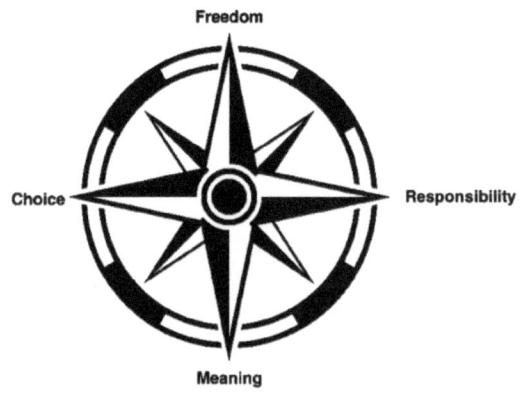

It answers four essential questions:
1. Who am I?
2. Why am I here?
3. What matters most to me?
4. How will I live that—every day?

This layer isn't about fixing pain.
It's about asking: Now that I'm no longer ruled by fear... what do I choose?

Scientific Insight: The Power of Meaning
Research in existential psychology and logotherapy (Frankl, 1959) shows that a strong sense of meaning:
- Increases resilience
- Reduces anxiety and despair
- Predicts long-term life satisfaction

Neuroscientific studies also show that purpose-driven living activates the brain's reward centers and reduces default mode overactivity—leading to more present-centered, value-integrated action (Park et al., 2010).

Freedom, Meaning, and Choice Across the Four Layers
True freedom is not the absence of limitation.
It's the presence of conscious, values-based direction—at every level.

1. Conscious Layer – Choosing How You Live
Symptoms of fragmentation:
- Life feels busy but empty
- Going through the motions
- Productivity without joy

Shifts:
- Time, energy, and attention integrated with values
- Saying no to say yes to what matters

Tools:
- Daily intention setting
- Time-audit based on purpose
- Values-driven routines

2. Preconscious Layer – Choosing What You Believe

Symptoms:
- "I don't know what I want."
- Internal conflict between desire and "shoulds"
- Subtle guilt for enjoying life

Shifts:
- Replacing inherited beliefs with chosen principles
- Identifying your actual priorities

Tools:
- Belief audit
- "Who says?" journaling
- Core value mapping

3. Unconscious Layer – Freeing What Was Fixed

Symptoms:
- Repeating old choices out of loyalty to pain
- Fear of becoming "someone else"
- Subconscious sabotage of joy

Shifts:
- Giving unconscious material a new job: from protection to integration
- Forgiveness of self and others

Tools:
- Parts work: "What does this part need now?"
- Dream re-authoring
- Letter to your younger self: "We're free now."

4. Existential Layer – Choosing Who You Are

Symptoms:
- Lack of meaning
- Restlessness despite success
- Questioning identity, direction, or contribution

Shifts:
- Freedom as responsibility
- Identity as active choice
- Meaning as something you create, not wait for

Tools:
- Logotherapy inquiry: "What is life asking of me right now?"
- Narrative identity writing: "The life I am here to live…"
- The Golden Rule Compass: "Would I want this done to me?"

Maya: So, this last layer…It's not about healing what was. It's about choosing what's next?

Dr. Elias: Exactly. The existential layer is not reactive. It's creative. It's where you stop asking, "What happened to me?" And start asking, "What do I want to stand for?"

Reflection Prompts
- What values do I want my life to express?
- What questions has my suffering invited me to ask?
- What does "freedom" really mean to me—right now?
- If I fully trusted my worth, what would I choose?

Implementation Tools
Tool 1: Daily Compass Check-In
Ask each morning:
1. What matters to me today?
2. How can I live that—in thought, word, or action?

End your day with:
- Did I live from my compass? If not, how can I realign tomorrow?

Tool 2: Narrative Identity Exercise

Write the story of your life—not as a biography, but as a mission:

"I am someone who was shaped by ____, chose to ____, and is here to ____."

Let it evolve as you do.

Tool 3: The Meaning Filter

Before making a decision, ask:
- Does this align with who I'm becoming?
- Does it serve fear—or freedom?
- Will I feel proud of this when I look back from the end of my life?

Commitment Statement

"I commit to living from my existential compass. I choose not just to heal, but to live on purpose. I am free—not because life is easy, but because I choose who I am, every day."

Maya: So, freedom isn't found. It's claimed.

Dr. Elias: Yes. It's remembered. It's created. And it begins the moment you decide to live as though your life matters—because it does.

Scientific References (Chapter 14)
- Frankl, V. E. (1959). Man's Search for Meaning.
- Park, C. L., et al. (2010). Meaning in life and adjustment to stress.
- Ryff, C. D. & Singer, B. H. (1998). The role of purpose in healthy aging.
- Schwartz, B. (2004). The Paradox of Choice.
- Deci, E. L., & Ryan, R. M. (2000). Self-determination theory and the facilitation of intrinsic motivation.

Chapter 15: Integration – A Life Remembered

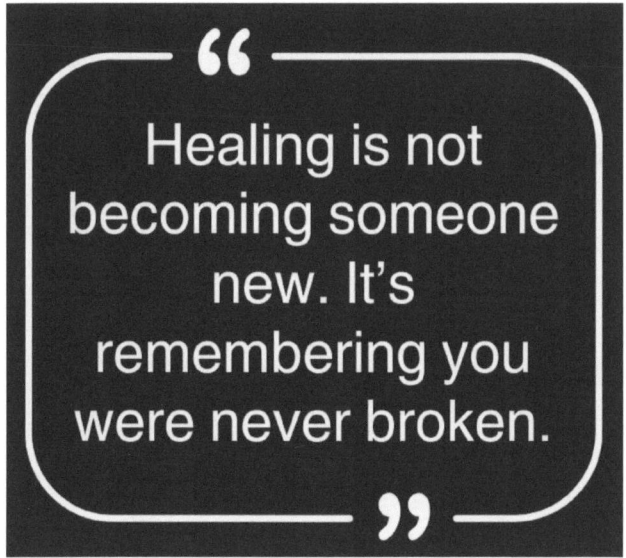

"Healing is not becoming someone new. It's remembering you were never broken."

Maya: *There's no grand finish, is there? No fireworks. Just… clarity. Peace. And this deep knowing: I'm home.*

Dr. Elias: *That's it. Integration isn't loud. It's the moment you realize you're no longer searching. You're being—fully, finally, freely.*

What Is Integration?

Integration is the lived experience of wholeness across all layers of your being.

It is when:
- Your actions (conscious)
- Your beliefs (preconscious)
- Your emotions and memories (unconscious)
- Your meaning and identity (existential)

…are no longer in conflict, but in coherence.

It is when you no longer forget who you are in the face of fear. When your life reflects your truth.

INTEGRATION CIRCLE

"The goal is not perfection. The goal is wholeness."

Scientific Insight: Integration and the Healing Brain

According to Daniel Siegel (2012), integration is the foundation of mental health. It occurs when different parts of the brain — especially the prefrontal cortex, amygdala, and hippocampus — work in harmony.

Integrated individuals demonstrate:
- Greater emotional regulation
- Increased self-awareness
- Stronger relationships
- Higher resilience under stress

Integration also mirrors secure attachment — within the self.

Integration Across the Four Layers

1. Conscious Layer – Daily Consistency

What it looks like:
- Your habits reflect your values
- Your presence is intentional
- You choose with clarity, not reactivity

Support Practices:
- Rituals
- Time-integrated to values
- Stillness and breath as daily anchors

2. Preconscious Layer – Belief Embodiment

What it looks like:
- Self-talk is kind and empowered
- Old patterns no longer run the show
- You catch the inner critic—and choose truth instead

Support Practices:
- Belief re-integration
- Daily affirmations based on chosen identity
- Reflective journaling to track shifts

3. Unconscious Layer – Integration of the Past

What it looks like:
- Your history no longer hijacks your present
- You hold space for inner parts with compassion
- Dreams offer guidance, not distress

Support Practices:
- Ongoing dream work
- Parts dialogue
- Periodic deep reflection or therapy check-ins

4. Existential Layer – Purposeful Presence

What it looks like:
- Your life has meaning—even when it's hard
- You choose how to respond, not just react
- You live by design, not default

Support Practices:
- Purpose journaling
- Compass check-ins
- Regular solitude to realign

Maya: So, remembering isn't just something I feel. It's something I live.

Dr. Elias: Yes. It's how you wake up. How you move through conflict. How you love. How you lead. How you return to yourself—again and again.

Reflection Prompts
- In what ways is my life already reflecting integration?
- Where do I still feel fragmentation—and what layer is asking for attention?
- What daily rituals help me stay connected to my remembered self?
- How will I know—from the inside—when I am living in integration?

Implementation Tools
Tool 1: The Integration Inventory (Monthly Practice)
For each layer, ask:
1. What's working?
2. What needs more attention?
3. What new action or insight is emerging?

Repeat monthly to track deep transformation.

Tool 2: The Remembering Ritual (Daily Anchor)

Each morning or evening, say aloud:

"I am whole. I am here. I am enough. I remember who I am."

Use breath, presence, and posture to embody the truth—not just speak it.

Tool 3: Integration in Action

Pick one ordinary activity (e.g., making tea, brushing teeth, walking).
Practice it as your remembered self.
Ask:
- How would I do this with presence?
- How would I do this as someone who knows: It's all perfect?

Over time, everything becomes sacred.

Commitment Statement

"I commit to living a life of integration, awareness, and purpose. I no longer seek wholeness—I choose to live it. I remember who I am."

Maya: So, this is it. Not a finish line—But a foundation.

Dr. Elias: Yes. The healing brought you here. But from here—you begin to truly live.

Scientific References (Chapter 15)
- Siegel, D. J. (2012). The Developing Mind.
- Schore, A. N. (2012). The Science of the Art of Psychotherapy.
- Van der Kolk, B. A. (2014). The Body Keeps the Score.
- Frankl, V. E. (1959). Man's Search for Meaning.
- Porges, S. W. (2011). The Polyvagal Theory.

Closing Poem

Before the Return

You thought you had to fix it all.
To figure it out.
To earn your way back.

But it was never about fixing.
It was about feeling.
It was about seeing.
It was about staying—even when it hurt.

You thought the healing would be louder.
More dramatic.
More certain.
But it came as a whisper,
as a breath,
as the quiet realization:
This, too, is part of it.

All of it.

The rising.
The falling.
The silence.
The fire.
The ache.
The opening.

You don't have to become someone new.
You only have to stop abandoning who you already are.

Because the truth is simple:
There was never anything wrong with you.
There was only forgetting.
And now…
there is remembering.

Let this be the moment you stop running.

Let this be the moment you say:
I'm home.

Epilogue: The Still Point

"There is a still point inside you that has never been afraid."

There is a place within you—
Untouched by time, trauma, or thought.
It is not your story.
It is not your symptoms.
It is not your conditioning.
It is the still point—
The place before perception. Before programming. Before pain.

You have touched it.

In stillness.
In surrender.
In those quiet moments when you stopped fighting and just were.

That still point is not a metaphor.
It is the most real thing about you.

It is the breath beneath the anxiety.
The presence beneath the persona.
The soul beneath the survival.

You don't need to become someone new.
You don't need to fix yourself.
You don't need to "do more" or "finally get it right."

You only need to return—again and again—to what has always been there.

The still point is where your preconditioned self waits with open arms.
It is where you remember:
It's all perfect.

Even the forgetting.
Even the falling.
Even this moment—right now.

So breathe.
Come home.
Live from this place.
And let your life speak not of striving, but of remembering.

Conclusion: There Was Never Anything Wrong With You

"You were not broken. You were buried."

This is not a book about becoming.
It's a book about returning.
Returning to the you that existed before fear, before performance, before programming.
The you who remembered that life is not a test, but a gift.
That pain is not punishment, but passage.
That every thought, every wound, every detour—was part of the curriculum of awakening.

There was never anything wrong with you.

You were shaped by what you didn't choose.
But now—you can choose.

You can choose to pause.
To breathe.
To walk differently.
To see yourself—and your life—not through the lens of trauma, but of truth.

You can live from the inside-out.
You can reclaim every layer—your actions, your beliefs, your buried voice, your chosen meaning.
You can live by your own compass.
You can let your life become a work of inner integration.
Not because everything is easy.
But because everything is yours now.

So take what you've remembered here…
And live it.

Let your habits reflect your truth.
Let your words carry your wholeness.
Let your relationships be spaces of presence, not performance.
Let your pain become purpose.
Let your life be your permission slip.

Because now you know:
It was always unfolding.
It was always part of the design.
And it was always—all perfect.

Invitation to the Reader

Dear Reader,

You made it to the end—but not the end of the journey.

In fact, what if this is the beginning?
The beginning of living your life differently—not as a problem to solve, but as a path to walk.
Not as something to fix, but as something to honor.
Not from fear—but from remembrance.

You don't need more information.
You need integration.
You need embodiment.
You need the quiet courage to live what you already know.

This book was not meant to be read.
It was meant to be practiced.

Reflection
So pause here.
Place your hand on your chest.
Feel your breath.
Ask yourself:
- What did I remember while reading this book?
- What old belief fell away?
- What new truth was born?
- What will I no longer abandon within myself?

This is your life.
This is your moment.
And you are no longer asleep.

Call to Action

Choose one thing—just one—that you will do today to live from the inside-out.

Maybe it's a breath.
Maybe it's a boundary.
Maybe it's choosing presence over panic, compassion over critique, surrender over control.

Then repeat tomorrow.
And the next day.
Until your whole life reflects the truth:
You were never lost. You were only remembering.

If you're ready to take this deeper, visit us at www.sweetinstitute.com to access free tools, join our healing community, or enroll in a course that will support your continued integration.

Because this journey doesn't end with a book.
It becomes a way of life.

Review Request

If this book moved you…
If you found yourself nodding, breathing deeper, or remembering something you didn't know you had forgotten—
Would you take a moment to leave a review?

Your words can help someone else say yes to their own healing. Your story can be the mirror they didn't know they needed.

Visit your favorite platform (Amazon, Goodreads, or anywhere books are shared), and let us know:
- What spoke to you?
- What shifted?
- What will stay with you long after the final page?

We read every review with gratitude.

And more than anything—we thank you.
For your courage.
For your presence.
For your part in this remembering.

With deep respect,
Mardoche Sidor, MD
Karen Dubin, Ph.D., LCSW
SWEET Institute

Final Acknowledgments

"If you made it here, it's because a deeper part of you always knew the way."

To every person who cracked open their heart in the reading of this book—we see you. We honor you. And we stand with you.

This is not the end of the conversation. It is the continuation of a movement:
To reclaim our truth.
To rewire what was once survival.
To restore what was always sacred.
To remember that it's all perfect—even the forgetting.

Thank you to the SWEET Institute team for holding the vision, building the scaffolding, and embodying the mission of healing through knowledge, presence, and radical love.

To our families, friends, and colleagues—you gave us the space and support to create. You gave us grace when we were writing instead of resting, dreaming instead of texting back. Thank you.

To the invisible hands—editors, designers, proofers, readers, and ancestors—thank you for holding this book through every layer of its becoming.

And to Life itself:
Thank you for unfolding exactly as you do.

In gratitude,
Mardoche Sidor, MD
Karen Dubin, Ph.D., LCSW
SWEET Institute

Reader Integration Toolkit

Practice. Presence. Remembering. Daily.

SECTION 1: DAILY ANCHORS FOR REMEMBERING

The 4-Layer Morning Check-In

Each morning, ask yourself:
- Conscious:
  What will I do today that aligns with my values?
- Preconscious:
  What belief will I choose to reinforce with my behavior?
- Unconscious:
  What emotion or memory is surfacing for attention?
- Existential:
  What kind of human do I choose to be today?

SECTION 2: WEEKLY PRACTICE FRAMEWORK

WEEKLY PRACTICE FRAMEWORK		
DAY	FOCUS	SAMPLE PRACTICE
Monday	Conscious Layer	Reorganize one habit to reflect your truth
Tuesday	Preconscious Layer	Journal a belief and its origin—then choose a new one
Wednesday	Unconscious Layer	Free-write for 15 minutes and circle recurring words or images
Thursday	Existential Layer	Ask: "What is life asking of me right now?"
Friday	Integration	Review the week. Where did you live from your center?
Weekend	Reflection & Rest	Nature walk, stillness, or creative play—no agenda but presence

SECTION 3: CORE TOOLS AND TEMPLATES

1. The Remembering Ritual (Daily Anchor)

Breathe deeply. Close your eyes. Place your hand on your chest.
Repeat aloud:

"I am whole. I am here. I am enough. I remember who I am."

Use it upon waking, in moments of overwhelm, or before sleep.

2. The "As If" Behavior Journal

Daily page for 7 days:
- What limiting belief showed up today?
- What behavior did I choose "as if" I were free?
- What did I learn from that action?
- How did it feel in my body?

3. The Belief Bridge Worksheet

- Current Belief:
  (e.g., "I'm not good enough")
- Bridge Thought:
  (e.g., "I'm learning to value myself.")
- Integrated Action Today:
  (e.g., "I spoke up in the meeting.")

Repeat until the new belief feels lived.

4. The Unconscious Uncovering Tool

- Sit quietly. Set a timer for 15 minutes.
- Begin free writing with:
  "What my unconscious is ready to show me is…"
- After, underline:
  - Symbols
  - Memories
  - Repeated phrases
- Circle one for deeper reflection or exploration in therapy.

5. The Existential Compass Template

Revisit weekly. Answer honestly.
- Who am I choosing to be this week?
- What value will guide my choices?
- What will I do with my freedom?
- What will I forgive in myself and others?
- What will I let matter most?

SECTION 4: MONTHLY INTEGRATION INVENTORY

Each month, reflect on the 4 layers:

MONTHLY INTEGRATION INVENTORY

LAYER	WHAT I'VE INTEGRATED	WHAT STILL NEEDS ATTENTION	NEXT INTEGRATED STEP
CONSCIOUS			
PRECONSCIOUS			
UNCONSCIOUS			
EXISTENTIAL			

SECTION 5: REMEMBERING ON THE GO

One-Line Guiding Principles (Repeat as needed):
- "This is not a mistake. It's an unfolding."
- "I am not my thoughts—I am the one who sees."
- "I don't have to rush. I only have to return."
- "Freedom is not the absence of fear. It's presence in the face of it."
- "Everything is part of the remembering."

Closing Prompt: Your Personal Integration Declaration

Write your own. Begin with:

"From this day forward, I choose to remember…"

Finish the sentence. Speak it aloud. Return to it often. companion for readers?

Appendices

Appendix A: Reader Integration Toolkit

Practice. Embody. Remember.

A1. Daily Four-Layer Morning Check-In

Start each day with these questions to stay integrated:
- Conscious Layer:
  What one action today reflects my values?
- Preconscious Layer:
  What belief am I reinforcing today?
- Unconscious Layer:
  What emotion, dream, or pattern is surfacing?
- Existential Layer:
  What kind of human do I choose to be today?

A2. Weekly Integration Practice

WEEKLY INTERGRATION PRACTICE

DAY	FOCUS	SUGGESTED PRACTICE
Monday	Conscious Layer	Restructure one routine to reflect your truth
Tuesday	Preconscious Layer	Journal a belief and challenge it with compassion
Wednesday	Unconscious Layer	Free write for 15–20 minutes
Thursday	Existential Layer	Ask: "What is life inviting me to become today?"
Friday	Integration	Reflect on the week: Where did I act from wholeness?
Weekend	Rest & Reflection	Walk, pause, reconnect without agenda

A3. Key Tools
The Remembering Ritual
Use each morning, during stress, or before sleep:

"I am whole. I am here. I am enough. I remember who I am."

Behavior–Belief Reflection Page
1. What belief showed up today?
2. What action did I choose despite it?
3. What does that action teach me about who I am?
4. What belief am I building now?

Belief Bridge Template
- Old Belief:
  e.g., "I'm not ready."
- Bridge Belief:
  e.g., "I'm learning to show up even when I'm scared."
- New Action Today:
  e.g., "I led the meeting anyway."

Free Association Prompt
Use for 15–20 minutes:

"What I've never allowed myself to say is…"
"What my unconscious is ready to show me is…"

Circle any recurring words, themes, or images for further reflection.

Existential Compass Check-In
1. What matters to me right now?
2. How will I act from that truth?
3. What kind of person am I choosing to become?

A4. Monthly Integration Inventory

MONTHLY INTEGRATION INVENTORY

LAYER	WHAT I'VE INTEGRATED	WHAT STILL NEEDS ATTENTION	NEXT INTEGRATED STEP
CONSCIOUS			
PRECONSCIOUS			
UNCONSCIOUS			
EXISTENTIAL			

A5. On-the-Go Guiding principles

- "This moment is not wrong."
- "I'm not behind—I'm on time for my own life."
- "I choose trust over control."
- "My life is not a performance. It's a practice."
- "I don't chase peace—I return to it."

A6. Your Personal Declaration

Complete this statement and revisit it often:

"From this day forward, I choose to remember…"

Let it guide you, ground you, and call you back to the still point inside.

Appendix B: Scientific References

This book is grounded in decades of research across psychology, neuroscience, trauma studies, and existential philosophy. Below is a list of core references cited throughout the chapters of It's All Perfect. These sources were selected to reflect the integration of scientific evidence and experiential healing that informs our 4-layer model of transformation.

Behavior, Thought, and Belief Systems
- Beck, A. T. (1976). Cognitive Therapy and the Emotional Disorders.
- Burns, D. D. (1980). Feeling Good: The New Mood Therapy.
- Clear, J. (2018). Atomic Habits.
- Festinger, L. (1957). A Theory of Cognitive Dissonance.
- Hayes, S. C., Strosahl, K. D., & Wilson, K. G. (1999). Acceptance and Commitment Therapy: An Experiential Approach to Behavior Change.

Trauma and the Unconscious
- Freud, S. (1900). The Interpretation of Dreams.
- Jung, C. G. (1964). Man and His Symbols.
- LeDoux, J. E. (2002). Synaptic Self: How Our Brains Become Who We Are.
- van der Kolk, B. A. (2014). The Body Keeps the Score: Brain, Mind, and Body in the Healing of Trauma.
- Young, J. E., Klosko, J. S., & Weishaar, M. E. (2003). Schema Therapy: A Practitioner's Guide.

Neuroscience and Integration
- Siegel, D. J. (2012). The Developing Mind: How Relationships and the Brain Interact to Shape Who We Are.
- Porges, S. W. (2011). The Polyvagal Theory: Neurophysiological Foundations of Emotions, Attachment, Communication, and Self-Regulation.
- Cozolino, L. (2010). The Neuroscience of Psychotherapy: Healing the Social Brain.
- Andrews-Hanna, J. R., et al. (2014). The brain's default network and its adaptive role in internal mentation.

Existential Psychology and Meaning-Making
- Frankl, V. E. (1959). Man's Search for Meaning.
- Seligman, M. E. P. (2002). Authentic Happiness: Using the New Positive Psychology to Realize Your Potential for Lasting Fulfillment.
- Deci, E. L., & Ryan, R. M. (2000). Self-determination theory and the facilitation of intrinsic motivation, social development, and well-being.
- Ryff, C. D., & Singer, B. H. (1998). The role of purpose in healthy aging.

Appendix C: Glossary of Key Terms

A guide to the core concepts and language of It's All Perfect. Use this glossary as a tool to reinforce your understanding and deepen your practice.

Belief Bridge

A transitional belief used to move from a limiting core belief to an empowering truth (e.g., "I'm not ready" → "I'm learning to trust myself").

Conditioned Self

The version of oneself shaped by fear, societal expectation, early survival strategies, and adaptive behavior. It is reactive, externally driven, and rooted in historical identity.

Existential Compass

The internal framework that helps individuals live with meaning, values, and freedom. It guides decision-making based on identity, purpose, and ethical integration.

Four Layers of Transformation

The core model used in this book:
1. Conscious Layer – Behavior, habit, structure
2. Preconscious Layer – Beliefs, emotional patterns
3. Unconscious Layer – Repressed emotion, memories, symbolic content
4. Existential Layer – Meaning, purpose, identity, spiritual truth

Free Association

A stream-of-consciousness practice that bypasses logic and control to access unconscious material. A tool for healing and remembering.

Integration

The process by which all parts of the self—across every layer—come into integration, coherence, and harmony. It's the lived experience of wholeness.

Preconditioned Self

The original, untainted self that existed before survival adaptations, trauma, or societal programming. It is whole, creative, peaceful, and wise.

Remembering

Not intellectual recollection—but spiritual, emotional, and somatic reconnection with one's essence. A return to the self before fear.

Schema

A deep, often unconscious mental framework created early in life that influences interpretation, emotion, and behavior (e.g., "I'm unworthy," "The world is unsafe").

Still Point

The inner place of peace, clarity, and presence that lies beneath thought, trauma, and ego. Accessible through breath, surrender, and silence.

Appendix D: Scientific Reference Index

Andrews-Hanna, J. R., et al. (2014). The brain's default network and its adaptive role in internal mentation. Trends in Cognitive Sciences, 17(10), 602–610.

Bargh, J. A., & Morsella, E. (2008). The unconscious mind. Perspectives on Psychological Science, 3(1), 73–79.

Beck, A. T. (1967). Depression: Clinical, Experimental, and Theoretical Aspects. New York: Harper & Row.
Beck, A. T. (1976). Cognitive Therapy and the Emotional Disorders. New York: International Universities Press.

Berne, E. (1964). Games People Play: The Basic Handbook of Transactional Analysis. New York: Ballantine Books.

Bowlby, J. (1988). A Secure Base: Parent-Child Attachment and Healthy Human Development. New York: Basic Books.

Brown, B. (2010). The Gifts of Imperfection: Let Go of Who You Think You're Supposed to Be and Embrace Who You Are. Center City: Hazelden.

Burns, D. D. (1980). Feeling Good: The New Mood Therapy. New York: Harper.

Clear, J. (2018). Atomic Habits: An Easy & Proven Way to Build Good Habits & Break Bad Ones. New York: Avery.

Cozolino, L. (2010). The Neuroscience of Psychotherapy: Healing the Social Brain. New York: Norton.

Deci, E. L., & Ryan, R. M. (2000). The "what" and "why" of goal pursuits: Human needs and the self-determination of behavior. Psychological Inquiry, 11(4), 227–268.

Festinger, L. (1957). A Theory of Cognitive Dissonance. Stanford, CA: Stanford University Press.

Frankl, V. E. (1959). Man's Search for Meaning. Boston: Beacon Press.

Freud, S. (1900). The Interpretation of Dreams. Standard Edition, Vols. 4 & 5. London: Hogarth Press.

Freud, S. (1915). The Unconscious. Standard Edition, Vol. 14.

Grupe, D. W., & Nitschke, J. B. (2013). Uncertainty and anticipation in anxiety: An integrated neurobiological and psychological perspective. Nature Reviews Neuroscience, 14(7), 488–501.

Hayes, S. C., Strosahl, K. D., & Wilson, K. G. (1999). Acceptance and Commitment Therapy: An Experiential Approach to Behavior Change. New York: Guilford Press.

Hayes, S. C., et al. (2006). Acceptance and commitment therapy: Model, processes and outcomes. Behaviour Research and Therapy, 44(1), 1–25.

Jacobson, N. S., Martell, C. R., & Dimidjian, S. (2001). Behavioral activation treatment for depression: Returning to contextual roots. Clinical Psychology: Science and Practice, 8(3), 255–270.

Jung, C. G. (1964). Man and His Symbols. New York: Dell.

Kihlstrom, J. F. (1987). The cognitive unconscious. Science, 237(4821), 1445–1452.

Kober, H., et al. (2010). Prefrontal-striatal pathway underlies cognitive regulation of craving. Proceedings of the National Academy of Sciences, 107(33), 14811–14816.

Langer, E. J. (1975). The illusion of control. Journal of Personality and Social Psychology, 32(2), 311–328.

LeDoux, J. E. (2002). Synaptic Self: How Our Brains Become Who We Are. New York: Viking.

Linehan, M. M. (1993). Cognitive-Behavioral Treatment of Borderline Personality Disorder. New York: Guilford Press.

Neff, K. D. (2003). Self-compassion: An alternative conceptualization of a healthy attitude toward oneself. Self and Identity, 2(2), 85–101.

Park, C. L., et al. (2010). Finding meaning in the face of loss: A longitudinal study of meaning-making and adjustment to bereavement. Journal of Consulting and Clinical Psychology, 78(3), 329–340.

Porges, S. W. (2011). The Polyvagal Theory: Neurophysiological Foundations of Emotions, Attachment, Communication, and Self-Regulation. New York: Norton.

Rizzolatti, G., Fogassi, L., & Gallese, V. (2004). Mirror neurons: From discovery to autism. Scientific American, 295(5), 54–61.

Rotter, J. B. (1966). Generalized expectancies for internal versus external control of reinforcement. Psychological Monographs, 80(1), 1–28.

Ryff, C. D., & Singer, B. H. (1998). The role of purpose in healthy aging: Evidence from epidemiological studies of well-being. In P. T. Costa & I. C. Siegler (Eds.), Recent Advances in Psychology and Aging, 75–94.

Schacter, D. L. (1999). The seven sins of memory: Insights from psychology and cognitive neuroscience. American Psychologist, 54(3), 182–203.

Schore, A. N. (1994). Affect Regulation and the Origin of the Self: The Neurobiology of Emotional Development. Hillsdale, NJ: Lawrence Erlbaum.

Schore, A. N. (2012). The Science of the Art of Psychotherapy. New York: Norton.

Seligman, M. E. P. (2002). Authentic Happiness: Using the New Positive Psychology to Realize Your Potential for Lasting Fulfillment. New York: Free Press.

Siegel, D. J. (2012). The Developing Mind: How Relationships and the Brain Interact to Shape Who We Are. New York: Guilford Press.

Skinner, B. F. (1953). Science and Human Behavior. New York: Macmillan.

White, M., & Epston, D. (1990). Narrative Means to Therapeutic Ends. New York: Norton.

Winnicott, D. W. (1960). The Maturational Processes and the Facilitating Environment. London: Hogarth Press.

Young, J. E., Klosko, J. S., & Weishaar, M. E. (2003). Schema Therapy: A Practitioner's Guide. New York: Guilford Press.

Zhang, D., & Raichle, M. E. (2010). The default mode network and self-referential processes in depression. NeuroImage, 52(4), 1231–1239.

Appendix E: Recommended Reading

Books to Deepen, Expand, and Sustain Your Journey of Remembering

On Healing and Trauma
- The Body Keeps the Score by Bessel van der Kolk, M.D.

  A foundational text on how trauma reshapes the body and brain—and how healing is possible through integration.
- Waking the Tiger by Peter A. Levine, Ph.D.

  An accessible introduction to somatic experiencing and how the body holds (and can release) trauma.
- Complex PTSD: From Surviving to Thriving by Pete Walker, M.A.

  A powerful guide to healing early developmental trauma and reconnecting with your authentic self.

On Thought, Belief, and Emotional Freedom
- Feeling Good: The New Mood Therapy by David D. Burns, M.D.

  A classic introduction to Cognitive Behavioral Therapy (CBT) and practical tools for reframing thought patterns.
- Radical Acceptance by Tara Brach, Ph.D.

  A compassionate invitation to embrace yourself—and all of life—with mindfulness and love.
- The Untethered Soul by Michael A. Singer

  An exploration of inner freedom, presence, and learning to observe the mind without being defined by it.

On the Unconscious and Inner Work
- Man and His Symbols by Carl G. Jung

  A rich introduction to Jungian psychology, dream work, and the symbolic language of the unconscious.

- Homecoming by John Bradshaw
  A healing journey to reclaim the inner child and release the burden of shame and family conditioning.
- The Wisdom of Your Body by Hillary McBride, Ph.D.
  An invitation to reclaim your body as a site of knowing, healing, and integration.

On Meaning, Purpose, and Existential Living

- Man's Search for Meaning by Viktor E. Frankl
  A timeless meditation on suffering, meaning, and the power of choice—even in the face of unimaginable pain.
- The Gifts of Imperfection by Brené Brown, Ph.D., LMSW
  A heartfelt call to live authentically, vulnerably, and wholeheartedly in a perfection-driven world.
- The Art of Happiness by His Holiness the Dalai Lama & Howard C. Cutler, M.D.
  A wise and accessible conversation on cultivating a meaningful life rooted in compassion.

On Integration and Inner Presence

- The Power of Now by Eckhart Tolle
  A modern spiritual classic on the transformative power of present-moment awareness.
- No Bad Parts by Richard C. Schwartz, Ph.D.
  An introduction to Internal Family Systems (IFS) and a pathway to healing inner fragmentation.
- In an Unspoken Voice by Peter A. Levine, Ph.D.
  A deeper dive into the neurobiology of trauma and the quiet, profound process of coming home to oneself.

Appendix F: Resources by the Authors

Continue your journey of healing, remembering, and integration

Books by the Authors

(Available on Amazon and at www.sweetinstitute.com)

- Before Anything Else, Validate (Upcoming)

    Learn how validation is the foundation of healing, connection, and transformation—in therapy, relationships, and leadership.

- The Power of Belief

    Discover how your core beliefs shape every area of your life—and how to change them for good.

- Breaking the Pattern (Upcoming)

    Explore the unconscious roots of repetition compulsion and how to interrupt painful cycles through deep internal work.

- How Life Works (Upcoming)

    A journey through the 20 universal life lessons that, when remembered, lead to peace, purpose, and personal power.

- The Kindness Imperative (Upcoming)

    A manifesto for heart-centered leadership, grounded in science, humility, and the power of grace.

Signature SWEET Institute Programs

- SWEET Healing Circles for Teams
  Five-hour immersive group experiences designed to activate healing across the four layers of transformation. Topics include:
    - Relationships
    - The Inner Child
    - Trauma and Integration
    - Remembering the Preconditioned Self
    - The Still Point
- The 10 Commitments Framework
  A step-by-step guide to consistent healing and sustained transformation. Includes daily practices, accountability systems, and integrative tools.
- Motivational Interviewing and Beyond
  A training series for clinicians and caregivers who want to embody therapeutic presence in every interaction—rooted in validation, attunement, and empowerment.

Ongoing Learning and Practice

- The SWEET Institute Membership
  Access to daily live seminars, certificate programs, coaching circles, and a private global community of clinicians and healing professionals.
- SWEET Institute Publishing
  Transformational books for a transformational world. Browse our full catalog or submit your manuscript at: www.sweetinstitutepublishing.com
- SWEET Think Tank
  An interdisciplinary community committed to advancing integrative healing and redefining systems of care through depth, presence, and practice.

Connect with the Authors

- Mardoche Sidor, MD

    Quadruple board-certified psychiatrist, founder of SWEET Institute, and pioneer of the 4-Layer Transformational Model.

    Follow: @drmardochesidor | www.sweetinstitute.com

- Karen Dubin, Ph.D., LCSW

    Social worker, co-founder of SWEET Institute, educator, co-author, and creative director at SWEET Institute Publishing.

    Follow: @drkarendubin | www.sweetinstitute.com

Free Downloads & Companion Materials (Upcoming)

Visit www.sweetinstitute.com/itsallperfect for:
- Printable versions of the Integration Toolkit
- Guided audio meditations
- Reflection journal prompts
- Companion videos for each chapter
- Live and on-demand workshops

About the Authors

Mardoche Sidor, M.D.

Dr. Mardoche Sidor is a Harvard- and Columbia-trained, quadruple board-certified psychiatrist with expertise in general psychiatry, child and adolescent psychiatry, forensic psychiatry, addiction psychiatry, community/public psychiatry, and Geriatric psychiatry. A teacher, mentor, and systems visionary, Dr. Sidor has dedicated his life to redefining what mental health care looks like—from the inside out.

He is the Founder of the SWEET Institute, a global learning and transformation platform for clinicians, educators, and leaders committed to sustainable healing through depth, presence, and practice. He previously served for eight years as an Assistant Clinical Professor of Psychiatry at Columbia University, where he helped train the next generation of physicians. He is currently affiliated with the Columbia University Center for Psychoanalytic Study and Research.

Dr. Sidor is the architect of the SWEET 4-Layer Model of Transformation, which integrates conscious behavior, core belief work, unconscious healing, and existential clarity to help individuals live a life of integration, purpose, and remembering.

Above all, Dr. Sidor believes that healing is not about becoming someone new—it's about remembering who you already are.

Karen Dubin, Ph.D., LCSW

Dr. Karen Dubin is a social worker, writer, educator, and the creative director at SWEET Institute Publishing. She holds a doctorate in Social Work and has spent over two decades helping individuals, clinicians, and communities transform their inner lives through insight, integration, and the power of presence.

With advanced training in trauma-informed care, depth psychotherapy, and narrative healing, Dr. Dubin is known for her poetic yet grounded approach to clinical work, always meeting people where they are—with dignity, wisdom, and love.

She is the Co-Founder of SWEET Institute, co-creator of SWEET Institute's Healing Circles, author and co-author of multiple transformational books, and a mentor to countless clinicians and caregivers who are reclaiming their work as a path of awakening.

Her work is rooted in the belief that every story holds a seed of liberation—and that remembering the truth of who we are is the most powerful form of resistance and healing.

www.ingramcontent.com/pod-product-compliance
Lightning Source LLC
Chambersburg PA
CBHW042308150426
43198CB00001B/3